WOMEN!

BEASTS OF BURDEN OR PARTNERS IN LIFE?

A comparative study of the status of women in the Judaeo-Christian and Islamic Scriptures

Naeem Osman Memon

WOMEN! BEASTS OF BURDEN OR PARTNERS IN LIFE?

By Naeem Osman Memon

FIRST BOOK EDITION: JANUARY, 2015

ISBN 978-0-9879611-1-2

Published by:

Insight360 Publishing
Web: http://www.insight360publishing.com
Email: info@insight360publishing.com

Dedicated to my blessed memory of my mother
Mahmuda Eshaq Osman.
May her soul rest in eternal peace!

ACKNOWLEDGEMENTS

Hadhrat Mirza Tahir Ahmad
Khalifatul Masih IV

and

Mr. Mostafa Sabit, Weston, Ontario, Canada
Mr. Eshaq Osman Memon, London, England
Mrs. Reema Shehzad Butt, Detroit, USA
Mrs. Amatul Rahman Osman, London, England
Mr. Azzeddine Ahmad Mustun, Curepipe, Mauritius
Mr. Adil Mahmood Osman, London, England
Mr. Shahbaz Jahangir Osman, London, England
Mr. Najm Shabih Naseer, London, England

Contents

PUBLISHERS NOTE

In the 1980s, the intensity of negative attitude in the media against Islam increased, speared on by world developments such as the Iranian revolution, the Gulf and Yugoslavian wars, Rushdie's publication of the Satanic Verses, the Afghan revolution and growing political disturbance in the Muslim world. Unbalanced and prejudiced reporting of events centred on the threat Islam, posed on the freedoms and safety enjoyed in Western societies. In addition, media stereotypes involving portrayal of Muslim women as passive victims of male power and criticism of Islam, for marginalising women and for providing a disproportionate amount of power to men, continued to emerge.

During this time, my father Naeem Osman Memon had been deeply engrossed in the study of theology and in particular Judaeo-Christian and Islamic faiths. Having written a number of books in this area he focused his attention to the writing of this book 'Women! *Beasts of Burden or Partners in Life'* in order to dispel the growing mischaracterisation of Islam in the area of women's status and rights and to help re-affirm Islam as the only major religion establishing a comprehensive set of laws governing rights women over 1400 years prior to Western countries which had only started establishing rights of women in past 100 years.

With my father's death in 1995 this book remained unpublished until now, nearly twenty years later. Over this time, Islam's stance on the treatment and rights of women further continues to be misrepresented by the media and, to a large extent, has resulted in negatively shaping public opinion with a large majority of society seeing Muslim ideology as a threat to Western ideals, peace and harmony. In this respect the need for a book such as this has never been more critical.

I want to take this opportunity to thank my brother Shahbaz, sister Mahvish, aunt Tahira and especially my wife Nosheen for their moral support in allowing me to finally publish this title and fulfil one of my father's final wishes.

Adil Osman Memon

CHAPTER ONE

UNIVERSAL ATTITUDE TOWARDS WOMEN

Since the earliest of times, man has yearned to cultivate a way of life which would make it easier for him to dominate the forces of nature and bring these under his control. In the beginning, he tilled the soil to grow crop and tamed rivers to cultivate land after which he turned his attention to lower creatures. He gained sufficient advantage over animals and domesticated these to serve his passion for sport and adventure and also assist him as beasts of burden. But his desire to gain supremacy did not satiate with the subjugation of virtually all the forces of nature nor did it slake with his subjection of God Almighty's creation of the lower order. Thus, he began to conspire against his other half - to bring her under his control and to effactually reduce her to a chattel owned by him.

The subjugation of the female species brought in its wake greater taboos which man had not anticipated when he initially embarked upon his mission to be the lord of the manor. But, this did not discourage him from pursuing his goal to exercise absolute power over God's entire creation. He imposed rules of social behaviour upon the female species which restricted its scope of action and movement and women were gradually forced into spending their lives confined to their homes as prisoners required to focus all their energy to the welfare of their masters and the households of their lords. They began to lead a life of physical drudgery, emotional servitude and spiritual deprivation and the only reward they could ever expect for their anguish and bondage was to win a right to the affection of their husbands, if they pleased them sufficiently.

The social stigma which eventually came to be attached to womanhood, coupled with the man's extremely possessive nature and excessive regard for his own honour eventually disrupted his peace of mind. He began to look upon the female species as a liability to an extent that in almost all known civilizations, the birth of a female offspring became a matter of grave concern and often grief and women came to be viewed as an evil necessity which man had to endure.

In the Babylonian society, they were reduced to a position of slaves and their only brief in life was to be mothers to their children and keepers of the household. If ever repudiated by their husbands, their only option was to become harlots and earn sufficient money to keep themselves alive. Although they enjoyed relative freedom from matrimonial bondage, yet they continued to be enslaved by their dependency on the male species to find them sufficiently attractive for illicit relationship.

The Egyptian women were also totally dependent upon their menfolk who subjected them to a great deal of physical drudgery and beating while denying them a right to redress. The Egyptian penal law itself showed great bias against the female species and punished wives for crimes committed by their menfolk. It required that if a husband be convicted of a crime, his wife share the burden of his sentence.

In the Greek civilization, women were considered inferior to their male counterparts and the Athenian Greeks brought up their daughters in strict seclusion with no more legal rights than those given to slaves. Athenian daughters were subjected to the authority of their fathers from whose legal guardianship they were passed unto the household of their husbands, only to spend their lives in self-denial. They became instruments of physical pleasure to their menfolk who were, for all practical purposes, considered their masters. In their conduct of war also, the Greeks showed singular bias against women. While male captives were permitted to be ransomed, female prisoners were enslaved to eternity - to become slave concubines expected to be available to their masters as well as gallant soldiers.

The Spartan Greeks did not treat their women any better since they considered the female species to be a mere instrument of human procreation. Wives unable to conceive a seed could expect to be divorced without compensation and forced to leave their matrimonial homes with absolutely nothing except that which their husbands had received from their in laws. They could also be lent to other men for extramarital relationships - particularly when a husband desired an heir and whereas a male issue could win the wife minimal respect, the birth of a female offspring could further hamper the mother's status and also the welfare of the infant daughter.

The Romans continued to hold their women in contempt. They considered their daughters mere chattels to be transferred to the ownership of their husbands who maintained that a wife's only duty was to bear children and take care of the household. The Roman law gave husbands a right to divorce their wives in the most unfortunate circumstances - such as infertility. Women were employed for sexual purposes in the homes of their masters as well as in brothels owned by them and girls were often sold by their parents or masters to be raised for the life of prostitution.

In China also, women were believed to be inferior to their male counterparts in every respect. Chinese men looked upon their daughters as a liability which, from the earliest age, was sold openly into houses of ill fame to be brought up for a life of depravity. If fortunate enough to be sought in marriage, brides suffered considerable humiliation at the hands of men who approached the entire issue of matrimony in an extremely business-like manner. They checked the credentials of their prospective brides in minor detail - to the point of humiliating physical examinations. Brides who passed the strenuous tests became principal wives to their husbands while their sisters and maids were secured as secondary wives and concubines. If ever divorced, Chinese convention stipulated that wives leave their matrimonial homes along with all the other women who accompanied them to the homes of their husbands.

In the Hindu culture, mothers generally looked upon their daughter as fellow sufferers born to eat the bread of affliction and drink the bitterness of tears. A Hindu woman's grief at the birth of a female offspring is beautifully depicted by a mother's lamentation:

> 'Better far, when life has been but one short cry, to end a doomed career in the tranquil waters of the river god, or quench by other means, a brand that, at best is only destined for burning. O Death! sighs a Hindu mother, I command my child to thee, for death is kinder to women than life.'

Unknown artist associated with William Carey (1761–1834) urporting to show infanticide committed by throwing an infant into the Ganges River

Hindu men considered the female species a liability and women in the household were often starved to feed the menfolk. Wives were subjected to the humiliation of being instruments of sexual gratification to several brothers of their husbands and sterile husbands could prevail upon them to perform the sacred conjugal rights of *niyog* with total strangers until a desired number of sons are born of such liaisons. Hindu women could also be pressurised by their spouses to perform *niyog* with as many as eleven strangers, one after another, while still serving the needs of their legal husbands. Widows were forbidden to remarry even if their marriages had not been consummated and the custom of *sati* often forced them to burn themselves to death on the pyre of their deceased husbands - failing which they could well expect to live a life of bare sustenance and public humiliation.

The Middle East also, was not immune to the universal custom of social degradation of the female species. The Judaic law expounded to Prophet Moses[as] did little to emancipate women who continued to remain a property of their fathers - only to be passed onto the ownership and household of their husbands where they mostly remained in subjection for the rest of their mortal lives. Scholars of religion have defined the 'relation of a Biblical wife to the husband as - for all intent and purposes, that of a slave and master.'

The advent of Christianity did little to lessen this burden imposed upon the female species by the Judaic law. In an exclusively Christian congregation, women were believed to have been created for the benefit of men and expected to remain in subjection to their fathers or their husbands until death did them part. They enjoyed minimal rights bestowed upon them by Biblical law but continued to live a life of physical drudgery, emotional pain and spiritual bondage as their spiritual predecessors did under Judaic conventions. With the expansion of Christian influence over gentile lands, the impositions placed upon women in Greek and Roman

6

cultures were replaced with the burden placed upon them by the Hebrew law and Paul's extension of it. Therefore, whatever little independence some women had acquired in these atheistic civilizations was lost on conversion to Christianity.

The other half of the patriarch Abraham's posterity - the pre-Islamic Arabs also held the female species in very low esteem and their attitude towards women was extremely unkind. Female infanticide was a common practice amongst the Arabs who looked upon their daughters as a financial liability and a possible source of disgrace and humiliation. Arabian daughters who survived this untimely death were subjected to severe physical and psychological humiliation. They could be sold to strangers or lost in a game of chance by their fathers or husbands. If fortunate enough to remain with their husbands until the death of their spouse, they were inherited by their step sons who could legally marry their own step mothers or else retain them as concubines. They could also be presented as a gift to other kinsmen of the heir or else be sold to strangers. Arabian wives could be made to perform conjugal rights with other men if their husbands were themselves sterile or desired an heir of noble extraction and women compelled into such arrangements were made to remain with these strangers until they conceived a seed and the signs of their pregnancy became apparent to the eye. Arabian convention also imposed polyandry upon women and a wife could be shared by as many as ten husbands while the husbands themselves practised unrestricted polygamy and even frequented brothels, maintaining a string of favourite whores. Such excessive indulgence did not restrict them from casual sex although they remained excessively jealous and protective of their honour when dealing with the conduct of their wives or concubines and even daughters or other women under their control.

Historical evidences therefore suggest that in nearly every known civilization, women have had to contend themselves with a woefully inferior status imposed upon them, not by an act of Divine will, but by their own menfolk. They have been deprived of every right as individual human beings while being subjected to extreme physical brutality by their more dominant menfolk. They have been required to endure severe emotional humiliation at the hands of their men who have traditionally treated the entire species as one of natures blunders but at the same time an essential evil which had to be tolerated in a society for the benefit of man. And, they have not only been considered to lack a soul, but often branded as agents of the devil. Since they were believed to be incapable of intellectual enlightenment or spiritual refinement, they were denied a right to exercise their potential towards higher spiritual pursuits. Although in certain ancient civilizations, some forceful women did manage to break this mould of subjugation, yet while worshipped as divine and immortal, they failed to demolish male prejudice against their species. For instance, the rules imposed upon a female deity's course of action restricted her a right to physical liaison with mortal males while male deities themselves enjoyed unrestricted choice amongst women of either status. A female goddess also lived her life in constant fear of physical abuse by both, immortal as well as mortal men while male gods remained free to entice, seduce or rape mortal as well as immortal women. This suggests that despite their allegedly divine status, women were viewed not as beasts of burden only but also objects of carnal indulgence and sexual gratification from the beginning of time.

CHAPTER TWO

THE JUDAEO-CHRISTIAN WOMEN

The Judaeo-Christian scriptures are probably the earliest sacred writings which recognise the female species as a human entity - subject to certain minimal rights. Yet, a woman does not have a place in Yahweh's original design since she is stated to have been conceived as an essential appendage to compliment His already planned creation. According to Biblical literature, God having created Adam in His own image and after His likeness[1] realised that it is not good that man should be alone.[2] Therefore, He decided to make Adam:

> **'an help meet for him. And out of the ground, the Lord God formed every beast of the field, and every fowl of the air, and brought them**

[1] Genesis 1.26/7
[2] Ibid., 2.18

> **unto Adam to see what he would call them: and whatsoever Adam called every living creature, that was the name thereof. And Adam gave names to all the cattle, and to the fowl of the air, and to every beast of the field: but for Adam, there was not found an help meet for him.3**

Adam was supposedly unable to find a suitable companion for himself among this large multitude of beast and fowl because 'he was not inclined towards bestiality and was thus able to determine that there was not a suitable companion for him among them.'4 Consequently, Yahweh proceeded to make other arrangements to fulfil His design and:

> **'The Lord caused a deep sleep to fall upon Adam, and he slept: and he took one of his ribs, and closed up the flesh thereof. And the rib, which the Lord had taken from man, made he a woman, and brought her unto the man.'5**

This legend of the earliest creation suggests that a woman was not a pre destined creation but an afterthought fashioned out of a man's rib. Therefore, she is not considered a distinct and independent entity but an essential appendage to God's already planned creation because she was created to fulfil the needs of the man whom the Lord had first created but had later decided not to leave alone.

The secondary status bestowed upon the Biblical women by the Hebrew Pentateuch finds considerable support in the exclusively Christian scriptures also which allege that a man, created by God in His own image and likeness:

---

3 Ibid., 2.18/20
4 Aid to Bible Understanding, Watch Tower Bible Society, p. 1664
5 Genesis 2.21/2

'is the image and glory of God: but the woman is the glory of man. For the man is not of woman; but the woman is of the man. Neither was the man created for the woman; but the woman for the man.'[6]

Apparently, such forceful scriptural argument in relation to the creation of the female species as a dependent entity have often led the Judaeo Christian clergy to relegate a woefully secondary and inferior status to women. They insisted that 'she was not originally created separately and although she was taken out of the man as a part of him, yet she is inferior to him because a man was not created for the woman's advantage but the woman for that of a man.'[7] This opinion is universally shared by Christian scholars of the Biblical scriptures who insist that since:

'a woman is from the man, she is on account of it inferior to him.'[8]

SUBJECTION TO MEN

The Biblical woman has thus been judged to have been created of the man and for him. Since she is stated to be entirely dependent upon the male species for her existence, she has traditionally been held as a secondary entity in the Judaeo Christian society and made subject to her other half - an eccentric subjugation argued to a degree where a comparison is drawn between its subjection to man in similar terms as the subjection of man to Christ and that of Christ to God. The New Testament states in relation to this:

---

[6] Corinthians 11.7/9
[7] Scott. Illustrated National Family Bible, p. 1106
[8] MacKnight. Illustrated National Family Bible, p. 1105

'know that the head of every man is Christ, and the head of the woman is the man and the head of Christ is God.'[9]

Consequently, the Christian scriptures demand of their women that they subject themselves to their men in everything just as they subject themselves to God or the Church subjects itself to Christ. They are admonished:

'Wives, be subject to your husbands, as to the Lord. For the husband is the head of the wife, as Christ also is the head of the Church, He himself being the Saviour of the body. But as the Church is subject to Christ, so also the wives ought to be to their husbands in everything. '[10]

Such admonitions are repeated often in the Biblical scriptures because women are stated to be subject to their menfolk by the Law[11] and because it is considered 'fitting in the sight of the Lord.'[12] Christian women are also directed to be subject to their husbands at home so 'that the word of God may not be dishonoured.'[13] This command is extended to also embrace husbands who are disobedient to the word of God[14] and spouses of a 'Gentile extraction or from amongst other unbelievers.'[15] These injunctions of the Biblical scriptures are justified on the ground that the

'man, being the image and glory of God has been appointed as His representative in ruling over this lower world and the woman, reflecting as it were, the man's glory and being the most

---

[9] 1 Corinthians 11.3
[10] Ephesians 5.22/4
[11] 1 Corinthians 14.34
[12] Colossians 3.18
[13] Titus 2.5
[14] 1 Peter 3.1
[15] Scott. Illustrated National Family Bible, p. 1174

honourable subject of his delegated authority ought to avow her willing subjection to him.'[16]

It is further argued that the 'man is the immediate head and ruler of the woman, to whose authority God has subjected her' and as such 'as Christ sought the honour of God, so the Christian should avow his subjection to Christ, doing his will and seeking his glory, and the woman should acknowledge her subjection to the man and do what is pleasing and honourable to him.'[17]

Apparently, these opinions in relation to the female species and its duties do not appear to have become antiquated with the process of time, even unto this day. Christian dogma in particular, continues to assert forcefully and often unashamedly that because:

'a woman was created out of a man, she is dependent upon him for her existence and being part of the man and also a complement and helper to him, she is subject to him as her head.'[18]

Whatever be the merits of these arguments, Biblical scriptures suggest that the subjection of the female species was a part of Yahweh's design who, from the earliest of times decreed that the man shall always rule over a woman. Thus, it was stated to her in the Hebrew Pentateuch:

'Thy desire shalt to be to thy husband, and he shall rule over thee.'[19]

---

[16] Ibid., 1106
[17] Ibid., 1105
[18] Aid to Bible Understanding, Watch Tower Bible Society, p. 1664 19. Genesis 3.16
[19] Genesis 3.16

CHATTEL OF SALE AND INSTRUMENT OF REWARD OR RANSOM

Since a woman is believed to have been created for a man as a compliment and helper for him and is required by the Biblical law to remain subject to him, in a Biblical society, a daughter remains the property of her father until she is given into marriage and he exercises an absolute right over her to deal with her in a manner he wishes or deems fit.[20] If he so desires, he may sell her into slavery - a permission granted to him by convention and the law itself which also stipulates that once sold into bondage, she may not be redeemed unless her purchaser initially designate her for himself and then find her displeasing to his eyes.[21]

A father may also pawn his daughters as security to relieve his own poverty and feed the rest of his family[22] and a daughter sold into slavery may either expect to be taken into the harem of her purchaser or be passed onto his male issue. She may be resold to a man of Hebrew stock or consigned to a Hebrew slave of her purchaser. If consigned to a fellow slave, her litter becomes the property of the master and unlike her male counterpart, neither she nor her children born in bondage possess the right to purchase their freedom. Nor is she permitted to accompany her enslaved partner on the expiration of his lawful bondage.[23]

Since Christian Scriptures maintain a total silence on the question of a father's right to sell his daughters into slavery in times of dire need, one may assume that these admit its legality through default or else it would have taken necessary steps to illegalise the permissibility of such disposal of the

---

[20] Aid to Bible Understanding, Watch Tower Bible Society, p. 423
[21] Exodus 21.7/8
[22] Nehemiah 5.5
[23] Exodus 21.4/9

female species by the Hebrew law of which the exclusively Christian scriptures are basically an extension.[24] Incidentally, this right given to Biblical men to sell female members of their own family is admitted by Christian scholars to have been exercised in Christian cultures until recently. It has been stated that:

'The right of the husband to sell his wife has been retained down to our own times.'[25]

A Judaeo-Christian father may, legally, use his chaste and virgin daughters as instruments of reward also. He may offer them as tribute to entice renowned soldiers to fight on his behalf[26] or as reward to total strangers to earn their support in times of need[27]- a tradition long known to Biblical convention and often practised in its history.[28] A daughter offered in such a deal is under obligation to accept her father's decision even if after offering her as reward for specific services to a particular person, he changes his mind and gives her unto another in breach of his promise.[29]

Sadly, this demand totally disregards the sentiments of women and forces them into a life of perpetual mental and emotional agony since the Hebrew Pentateuch confines the right of divorce to the husband[30] while the Christian scriptures deny women a right to seek divorce[31] and insist that the wives remain married to their husbands[32] because they are bound to them by the Law until death does them part.[33] Therefore, a woman traded into matrimony by her father has to spend

---

[24] Matthew 5.17/19
[25] Emerson, Ralph Waldo, English Traits
[26] 1 Samuel 18.17
[27] Ibid., 17.22/5
[28] Joshua 15.16/17
[29] 1 Samuel 18.17/19
[30] Deuteronomy 24.1/4
[31] Mark 10.12
[32] 1 Corinthians 7.10/11
[33] Romans 7.2

the rest of her life with a husband imposed upon her - whether she is able to reconcile to him as her partner in life or not.

If circumstances demand, Judaeo Christian daughters may be found sufficiently expendable to be offered as ransom to perverts, to protect the honour of men or else be thrown to a mob as substitute to save the male species from being sexually abused by depraved men. A father has the right to permit a degenerate crowd to deal with his chaste and virgin daughters as it deem fit as long as his male guests are spared humiliation. He is entitled to plead:

> **'Behold now, I have two daughters which have not known man: let me, I pray you, bring them out unto you, and do ye to them as is good in your eyes: unto these men do nothing.'**[34]

The arbitrary right to subject chaste and virgin women to physical violation, emotional humiliation and psychological distress by perverts is justified by Biblical exegesis on the grounds that:

> **'The sacredness of the rites of hospitality may be pleaded in its palliation.'**[35]

An honourable thought indeed, but, an excuse of this nature neither extenuates the ignominy of the offer nor does it mitigate the seriousness of the offence. It also holds women in great contempt and defines them as expendable objects which may be sacrificed at the altar of man's false sense of duty and honour. Moreover, the validity of such an excuse is far from being established since the purpose of such an exercise is not to protect the rights of hospitality but the honour of male guests threatened with sexual abuse. This is

---

[34] Genesis 19.8
[35] Turner, Illustrated Nat. Family Bible, p. 18

borne by the fact that when a host is confronted with an emergency of this nature, Biblical conventions find it permissible for him to implore the mob to spare his male guest with the plea:

> **'Nay my brethren, nay, I pray you, do not so wickedly seeing that this man is come into my house, do not this folly. Behold, here is my daughter, a maiden, and his concubine; them will I bring out now, humble ye them, and do with them what seemeth good unto you: but unto this man do not so vile a thing.'**[36]

Such pleas should sufficiently establish that the primary purpose of this offer is not to protect the sacred rites of hospitality but the honour of the host and his male guest - else the host would offer his own daughter only to the depraved mob and not the distressed female concubine of his male guest also, who, within her own right, is also a guest entitled to the same rites of hospitality as her husband. Yet, while the male guest is entitled to protection within the four walls of the host's house in relative security, the bewildered and frightened female guest can be seized and brought forth unto the depraved mob who may abuse her physically and rape her all night and finally throw her at the doorway of her host's house at dawn.[37]

A man not threatened by such an exigent situation which requires sacrifice at the altar of the sacred rites of hospitality may also offer women under his charge to be similarly assaulted and violated.[38] Apparently, he is permitted to do this because he is believed to have a divine right to protect himself at the cost of the physical, emotional and spiritual

---

[36] Judges 19.23/4
[37] Ibid., 19.25/6
[38] Judges 19.25

welfare of his wife. Judaeo Christian apologists maintain that a husband threatened with sexual violence by a mob may:

> **'in the hour of danger, apparently to save his own life, determine to sacrifice his wife and suffer her to be brought out and be exposed to the fiends in human shape.'**[39]

A divine right to sacrifice his own wife, a Biblical husband probably has. This is indicated by the fact that the Law makes no attempt to forbid him from such an act nor hold him responsible for the fate suffered by his wife if he decides not to follow the mob to save her from being abused out of 'fear lest the mob should do him a mischief.'[40] Nor does it demand retribution from him or punish him if he deliberately murders his defiled wife after the unfortunate woman has been abused by the mob[41] even though it demands that 'a murderer shall surely be put to death.'[42] On the contrary, a husband who throws his wife to a mob to save himself from being sexually humiliated and, then proceeds to mercilessly butcher her after she has been physically violated is able to solicit the sympathy of nearly the entire nation which is required to assist him to avenge the humiliation suffered by him.[43] Yet, at no stage is he required to answer for his own conduct in so much that in murdering an innocent woman for no offence on her part, he has infringed the 6th Commandment[44] for the violation of which the Law prescribe a penalty of death.[45]

Some Christian scholars shroud this ignominious right given to men with the pretext that 'the low estimate in which the female character was held in ancient times may be pleaded

---

[39] Bush. National Family Illustrated Bible, p. 283
[40] Henry. National Family Illustrated Bible, p. 283
[41] Judges 19.28/9
[42] Numbers 35.16/18
[43] Judges 20.1/24
[44] Exodus 20.13
[45] Numbers 35.16/18

in palliation of this abominable offer.'[46] But this excuse is as delusive as the one in relation to the sacredness of the rites of hospitality since such odious offers are not known to have been made in ancient history only but also recorded in the history of the Judaeo Christian nation after the Law had been expounded[47] - the law which did not restrict a man's right to subject his wife to physical abuse and psychological distress at the hands of depraved mobs to either save himself from being sexually abused or else protect his own honour. Since the entire Hebrew charter remains silent on the question of a man's right to sacrifice his wife at the altar of his personal honour and does not restrict this ancient Biblical convention, it gives him a right by default to deal with her in a manner he finds comfortable or expedient. And because this right has not been denied to men in the exclusively Christian congregation, one could safely assume its permissibility in the Christian faith also as the Hebrew Pentateuch constitute a part of the Christian scriptures and an extension of its Law.[48]

SPIRITUAL DOMINATION OF FEMALES

Apparently, the reason why Biblical literature does not address itself to this problem may be explained by the low esteem in which the female species has been held by the Bible in every sphere of human life. A man does not only possess an absolute control over a woman's physical being which entitles him to submit her to physical humiliation if circumstances demand, but he also exercises an autocratic control over her spiritual welfare. A father may, with full sanction of the Law, intrude upon his daughter's right to spiritual discipline and deny her freedom to independent spiritual engagement and a daughter who has pledged herself

---

[46] Turner. Illustrated National Family Bible, p. 18
[47] Judges 19.1/30
[48] Matthew 5.17/19

to some spiritual exercise without his knowledge may expect her vows to be annulled by him. The Bible gives the father authority to disallow his daughter a right to honour her vows and if he decides to encroach upon her resolve, she is obliged to sustain his decision since the Law demands:

> **'If a woman also vow a vow unto the Lord, and bind herself by a bond, being in her father's house in her youth; and her father hear her vow, and her bond wherewith she hath bound her soul, and her father shall hold his peace at her; then all her vows shall stand, and every bond wherewith she hath bound her soul shall stand. But if her father disallow her in the days he heareth; not any of her vows, or her bonds wherewith she hath bound her soul, shall stand; and the Lord shall forgive her, because her father disallowed her.'[49]**

Such domination of Judaeo-Christian women in the realm of their spiritual life continues even after they are released from paternal bondage through matrimony. This merely entails a transfer of ownership and a married woman is under the same obligation to her husband as her unmarried counterpart is to her father. The Law permits a husband to exercise a despotic control over his wife's spiritual conduct and action in life. It states that:

> **'If she had at all a husband when she vowed, or uttered ought out of her lips, wherewith she bound her soul; and her husband heard it, and held his peace at her in the day that he heard it; then her vows shall stand, and her bonds wherewith she bound her soul shall stand. But if**

---

[49] Numbers 30.3/5

> her husband disallowed her on the day he heard
> it, then he shall make her vow which she had
> vowed, and that which she uttered with her lips,
> wherewith she bound her soul, of none effect.'[50]

These stringent injunctions continue to be upheld in the exclusively Christian congregation which does not endeavour to break this mould of female subjugation to sufficiently liberate its women. On the contrary, Christianity encourages this subjection of women by demanding of the Christian wives:

> 'Submit yourselves unto your husbands, as unto
> the Lord. For the husband is the head of the
> wife, even as Christ is the head of the church;
> and he is the saviour of the body. Therefore, as
> the church is subject to Christ, so let the wives be
> to their husbands in everything.'[51]

It is, therefore, an essential part of the Christian faith that a woman continue being subject to her husband since this domination of the female species by its menfolk in a Judaeo-Christian civilization has the sanction of the Biblical law which demands:

> 'Know ye not, brethren, for I speak to them that
> know the law, how that the law hath
> domination over a man as long as he liveth? For
> the woman which hath an husband is bound by
> the law to her husband so long as he liveth.'[52]

Consequently, a Christian woman is required to maintain an extremely low profile throughout her life and rely upon the goodwill of the male species in all spheres of her life, physical

---

[50] Ibid., 30.6/8
[51] Ephesians 5.22/4
[52] Romans 7.1/2

21

as well spiritual. In fact, the Biblical law goes to the extent of even denying her a human being's most basic and fundamental right, that to free speech and demands:

> **'Let the woman learn in silence with all subjection. But I suffer not a woman to teach, nor usurp authority over the man, but be in silence'**[53]

This injunction stipulates that women do not even enquire of matters relating to their spiritual welfare except of their husbands and requires that if they fail to understand anything of religious importance, they not request that the matter be further elaborated and explained to them in public by their spiritual guides and counsellors. Such demands are made upon women because it is considered shameful for them to speak in public and Christian husbands are admonished:

> **'Let your women keep silence in the churches: for it is not permitted unto them to speak; but they are commanded to be under obedience, as also saith the law. And if they will learn anything, let them ask their husbands at home; for it is a shame for women to speak in the church.'**[54]

The gag put on a woman's right to free speech, even in matters of religious interest, is justified in Paul's epistles on the grounds that:

> **'Adam was first formed, then Eve. And Adam was not deceived, but the woman being deceived, was in transgression.'**[55]

---

[53] Timothy 2.11/12
[54] 1 Corinthians 14.34/5
[55] 1 Timothy 2.13/14

RIGHT TO INHERITANCE

Since Biblical literature considers women the property of either their fathers or their husband, it denies them a right to inherit property from the estate of their fathers or husbands as well as their children. Its laws require transfer of inheritance to male offsprings only, and women are entitled to the estate of their deceased father under exceptional circumstances, that is, when there are no male issues amongst whom his wealth can be distributed. The Bible states that if a Judaeo-Christian:

> 'man die, and have no sons, then shall ye cause
> his inheritance to pass unto his daughters.'[56]

Apparently, this provision granted to the daughters of a deceased under exceptional circumstances had not been thought of until some extremely outspoken and head strong Hebrew daughters refused to be intimidated by the dominant men in their society and they approached Moses with a complaint as to why should the name of their 'fathers be done away from among his family because he hath no son.' Consequently, Moses brought their case before Yahweh who saw wisdom in the complaint being made by these women and the Biblical law of inheritance was thereafter, slightly modified to make some concession to the female species.[57]

Yet, although it permitted distribution of a deceased's wealth to his female offsprings under such unavoidable circumstances, the permission itself was not granted in consideration of the rights of women. It was merely designed to protect male interest and, in this instance, the name of a male, the deceased father, from being blotted out from amongst his people. This is evident from the fact that these

---

[56] Numbers 27.8
[57] Ibid., 27.4/7

23

women whose complaint brought about a minimal relaxation in the Biblical law of inheritance did not seek to inherit the property of their father on the grounds as to why should they, being of the female species be disinherited. The premise of their objection was that there should be 'no cause as to why the name of their father should be done away from among his family if because he died without a male issue'[58] and, the Lord, having considered their objection:

> **'spake unto Moses, saying, the daughters of Zelophehad speak right.'[59]**

Yet, while Yahweh accepted the argument of these extremely bold Hebrew women and permitted them to inherit the property of their father in absence of an option, the Law imposed some very stringent conditions on them in so much that they were denied a right to marry outside the tribes of their father. It stated:

> **'Let them marry to whom they think best; only to the family of the tribe of their fathers they shall marry.'[60]**

Consequently, the restriction which denied the daughters of Zelophehad a right to free choice in marriage became an integral part of the Biblical law of Inheritance and the Bible states that:

> **'Every daughter, that possesseth an inheritance in any tribe of the children of Israel, shall be wife unto one of the family of her father.'[61]**

These conditions have been placed upon the female species to once again protect male interest so that the legacy of the

---

[58] Ibid., 27.1/4
[59] Ibid., 27.6/7
[60] Ibid., 36.6
[61] Ibid., 36.8

children of Israel may not be taken away from the inheritance of men and:

'**that the children of Israel may enjoy, every *man* the inheritance of his father.'[62]**

Biblical bias against the right of women to inherit property from their fathers and other male relatives is more than evident from the fact that where, in the absence of male issues, there are also no daughters to inherit the deceased's estate, his wealth is distributed amongst his brothers. And, if there be no brothers also, then the property is distributed among the brothers of the deceased's father failing which his entire estate is distributed to the person's:

'**kinsmen that are next to him of his family.'[63]**

But, it is never distributed amongst his kinswomen who may have much closer ties to the deceased, as for instance, a widowed wife who could have spent a greater part of her life with him, or a mother who bore in pain and nourished him to adulthood and even sisters who may be alive and better entitled to the wealth of their deceased kinsman.

The height of injustice occasioned to the female species by the requirement of the Biblical law of inheritance is that the widow of a deceased cannot, within her own right, inherit the property of her departed husband. Thus, a Judaeo-Christian widow stands to lose everything, including her matrimonial home and financial security if ever her spouse dies leaving her childless. Under such unfortunate conditions, the Law prevails upon the distressed widow to subject herself to a levirate marriage with her deceased husband's brother and

---

[62] Ibid., 36.8
[63] Ibid., 27.9/11

the first born son of this arrangement inherits the property of his mother's deceased spouse.[64]

But, a levirate marriage may not be possible on account of several factors. The widow's husband could have been the sole or only surviving male issue of his father and in which situations, she could be made to return to her paternal home.[65] If out of loyalty to her husband's family she pleads permission to remain with her in-laws and they are compassionate enough to allow her to remain with them[66], she could temporarily enjoy the benefits of her deceased husband's wealth but in trust only until it can be eventually redeemed by a male relative of the deceased. And, if ever redeemed by one, the widow herself would become the property of the male purchaser who redeems her deceased husband's estate.[67]

A levirate marriage may also not be possible if the surviving brothers of the deceased husband have not attained age of puberty. The widow could then be ordered to return to her father's home to await puberty of her father in-law's minor sons and while she is under legal obligation to remain bound to her deceased husband's family even if arrangements for her financial welfare have not been made, her father in-law may have absolutely no intention to accept her back into the family through a levirate marriage with any one of his surviving sons. Thus, she could be deprived of the estate of her deceased husband.[68]

She could also be deprived of her departed husband's wealth through the scheming of her brother in law, if accepted as a leviratical wife by one, since she remains at the mercy of this husband imposed upon her to show compassion towards her

---

[64] Deuteronomy 25.5/6
[65] Ruth 1.8/15
[66] Ibid., 1.16/22
[67] Ibid., 4.1/13
[68] Genesis 38.11

and not become engaged in schemes to ensure that she is unable to conceive an issue within the levirate marriage. Otherwise, she may well expect to bid farewell to the estate of the deceased husband as she may never conceive a seed and thereby establish her claim to his wealth.[69]

Ironically, the Biblical law fails to make satisfactory arrangements to restore the wealth of a deceased husband to his widow under such exigent circumstances while, in the meantime, she either burdens the financial resources of her parent's home or begins to live a life of a pauper, dependent upon hand-outs and even turn to adultery and conceive an illegitimate seed to demand her right.[70]

SCRIPTURAL BIAS AGAINST WOMEN

Biblical ordinances on tort and offenses against persons appear to be sufficiently strict and penalties for transgression excessively harsh. Yet, these display a singular bias against the female species. Although, the Law against promiscuity ordains that if a man is found lying with a married woman or a virgin engaged to be married then both of them ought to be put to death[71], this apparently equitable sentence imposed upon both offenders ought not to be seen as evidence of impartial treatment of the sexes. These ordinances are, in essence, designed to exclusively protect the interests of men to whom these women in question belong - the husband of the married woman or the fiancé of the virgin engaged to be married. This is clearly indicated by the reasons given for punishing the man which suggest that the offending male is not being punished because he committed the abominable sin of adultery but, as stated by the Bible:

---

[69] Ibid., 38.9
[70] Ibid., 38.14/18
[71] Deuteronomy 22.22/4

'because he hath humbled his neighbours wife; so shalt thou put away evil from among you.'[72]

The fact that an adulterer is punished in Biblical law because he commits a trespass against another man's rights and not because of the offence itself is also indicated by the diversity of punishment prescribed for similar offenses in which the rights of other men are involved as against those in which the rights of a husband or fiancé are not involved. One would expect that a male offender who forcefully violates a chaste virgin not engaged to be married to another man[73] would be expected to receive a much harsher punishment than a man who seduces a married woman and commits adultery with her with the consent of the woman involved.[74] Yet, in situations where a man commits adultery with consenting adult women who belong to another man, he is sentenced to death[75] while a rapist who forcefully defiles a chaste and unattached virgin against her will is able to atone his crime and secure his life with a token penalty of fifty shekels of silver despite his unwarranted attack on an innocent and unwilling woman.[76]

Biblical punishments being more severe in cases of adultery where the rights of other men are infringed than in cases where the rights of other men are not breached is illustrated by yet another comparison. The Law requires that a man who forcefully dishonours a woman engaged to another man ought to be sentenced to death because he has defiled the property of her fiancé husband and humbled his neighbour's bride to be.[77] Yet, a man who forcefully violates the chastity of a virgin who is neither married nor engaged to another

---

72 Ibid., 22.24
73 Ibid., 22.28
74 Ibid., 22.22
75 Ibid.
76 Ibid., 22.28/9
77 Ibid., 22.25

man is permitted to go away with a relatively low and token penalty of fifty shekels of silver to be paid to her father because in this instance the rights of another man, a husband or a fiancé, have not been ravaged. The Law states in relation to this:

> **'If a man find a damsel that is a virgin, which is not betrothed, and lay hold of her, and lie with her, and they be found; then the man that lay with her shall give unto the damsel's father fifty shekels of silver and she shall be his wife.'[78]**

One could argue that in violating the chastity of the virgin, the offender abuses the rights of her father and, therefore, the interests of a male have in one way or another been infringed. But one observes that Biblical ordinances compensate the father with fifty shekels of silver for his property which stands ravished - in this instance the virginity of his daughter. Therefore, the owner of the defiled virgin is compensated with the payment of the bride price which is all he could have expected if his daughter were to be married with her virginity intact, that being the Law:

> **'If a man entice a maid that is not betrothed, and lie with her; he shall surely endow her to be his wife. If the father utterly refuse to give her unto him, he shall pay money according to the dowry of virgins.'[79]**

The abused woman on the other hand does not receive compensation nor does she see justice being done and her assailant punished for depriving her of something which most righteous women cherish - their virginity and consequently their honour and respect. In fact, while her male owner, the

---

[78] Ibid., 22.28/9
[79] Exodus 22.16 Deuteronomy 22.29

father is compensated for the tragedy which his defiled daughter has had to suffer and endure, the innocent female victim is forced into a situation where she may well expect to be humiliated for the rest of her life by the culprit who initially abused her physically; robbed her of her virginity; deprived her of her state of chastity and purity and dented her honour and self-respect. Biblical law stipulates that she be given in marriage to her assailant who, in the first instance committed an offence against her body and soul - to be violated by him with the full sanction of the Law for the rest of her life since it does not permit women to seek divorce and it in such instances, it also binds husbands 'not to put their wives away for the rest of their mortal lives.'[80]

These Biblical injunctions not only disregard the pain and agony suffered by innocent women when they are first raped and humiliated but effectually throw them to the mercy of their assailants, to be constantly humiliated and violated by them. These poor victims of man's physical passions and sexual lust are made to constantly carry the burden of their unpleasant and tragic past throughout their life. They are reminded of it whenever they lay sight on these husbands imposed upon them by the Law and they cannot but suppress the memory of their traumatic experience whenever approached by them. They become virtual prisoners to this shocking experience and rather than assist them in forgetting the calamity which befell them, Biblical law keeps the thought of their traumatic experience alive for them by forcing them into an eternal bond of matrimony with their assailants. Alas! these unfortunate women carry the memory of their anguish and trauma to their graves.

It is further observed that Biblical ordinances totally disregard the rights and emotional susceptibilities of other women affected by this unwarranted and abominable act of the

---

[80] 16 Deuteronomy 22.29

offending male. The culprit may quite possibly be a married person and, as such, a husband who infringes the rights of his lawful spouse by lying with a woman that is not his lawfully wedded wife. The most bizarre aspect of this entire farce is that while the legal spouse has no recourse to demand retribution from her husband for violating the sanctity of her marriage, she is obliged to accept another woman in her household and share her husband with a person unlawfully violated by him but then given unto him to wife as part of his punishment - a punishment which one is certain, an evil man capable of committing such an abominable offence would not begrudge.

This singular bias against the rights of women in the Judaeo-Christian scriptures is admitted without apology in the exclusively Christian congregation also on the grounds that:

'for a married man to lie with a single woman was not a crime of so high a nature.[81]

In sharp contrast to this, Biblical ordinances demand that if a woman is violated by another man before she is married and is later accused of being a defiled person by her husband, then she is to be condemned to death. The Bible states that if a husband accuses his wife of not being a virgin and:

'if this thing be true, and the tokens of virginity be not found for the damsel: then they shall bring out the damsel to the door of her father's house, and the men of her city shall stone her with stones that she die; because she hath wrought folly in Israel, to play a whore in her father's house: so shalt thou put evil away from among you.'[82]

---

[81] Henry. Illustrated National Family Bible, p. 215
[82] Deuteronomy 22.20/1

Rembrandt's depiction on the practice of stoning to death women charged with adultery

This requirement of the Law discriminates against the female species in so much that the man who defiles a chaste and single woman is not considered to have committed a crime of such a high nature - irrespective of the fact that an abominable offence of unlawful sexual activity may have been committed by him with brute force. But a woman guilty of the same offence with a consenting male and without any violence is stated to have wrought folly in Israel and played a whore in her father's house because it is maintained that:

'If the uncleanliness was committed before she was betrothed she must die for the abuse she put upon him whom she married.'[83]

An excuse of this nature is in itself an admission of the fact that every punishment meted upon the offender by Biblical ordinances is in consideration of the harm that has been brought upon men in the Judaeo-Christian society, whether these be husbands or husbands to be of the women involved, and not in consideration the offence committed by the male offender - irrespective of the enormity of the person's conduct and action.

PARTIAL LAW OF RETRIBUTION

Biblical scriptures show extreme bias against women in its law of Divine retribution which treats women with singular prejudice. A woman accused of not being a virgin by her husband at the time of her marriage is condemned to death if proven to have been a defiled person at the time of her marriage. The Law states that if her husband's allegations against her be true:

---

[83] Henry. Illustrated National Family Bible, p. 215

> 'then they shall bring out the damsel to the door
> of her father's house, and the men of her city
> shall stone her with stones that she die; because
> she hath wrought folly in Israel, to play a whore
> in her father's house: so shalt thou put evil away
> from among you.'[84]

Yet, while she is accused of having played a harlot and condemned to death, the Biblical code of conduct makes no attempt to seek and punish the male offender who had been an equal party to the offence. It remains silent on this question and thus, by default, allows the offending man to continue his life without fear of being similarly punished for having committed an enormity of the same proportion for which the female party is condemned to death.

Similarly, a man who forcefully ravishes a virgin not engaged to another man is also able to atone his sin with a token penalty of a bride price to be paid to the maiden's father which also secures a bride for him - to legally possess and lawfully abuse for the rest of her mortal life. The Bible state in relation to this:

> 'If a man that find a damsel that is a virgin,
> which is not betrothed, and lay hold of her, and
> lie with her, and they be found, then the man
> that lay with her shall give unto the damsel's
> father fifty shekels of silver, and she shall be his
> wife, because he hath humbled her, he may not
> put her away all her days.'[85]

In both these situations women are seen to suffer grave consequences whether they are guilty of a deliberate offence or not. They are either condemned to death and deprived of life if found guilty or else, if innocent, thrown to the mercy of

---

[84] Deuteronomy 22.13/21
[85] Ibid., 22.28/9

34

their assailant while the offending men, positively guilty of a heinous sin in both situations, are either permitted to remain anonymous or be rewarded with a bride. In addition to this, the law of divine retribution slights the infringement of the divine code by the offending men and continues to bestow greater bounty and reward unto them. Although they totally disregard the laws of morality and indulge in crimes of carnal passion, they are permitted to atone their breach with verbal confession even if their sin be as enormous as incest.[86] Thereafter, they continue to be recipients of untold divine blessings which are also passed unto their future generations.[87] They are also able to expiate their transgression, as grievous as wilful ravishment of another man's wife[88] with verbal confession of their sin and they are not only pardoned, but their lives are, allegedly, extended by an act of divine will for them to make amends.[89] Apparently, they live to see great bounty bestowed upon them by divine will - only to die in the fullness of age with great honour.[90]

Yet, the same divine law of retribution exacts instant and vengeful retribution from women for their trespass of the moral code. A woman who defiles her husband's bed, but, is pardoned by him and restored to her former status by her spouse[91] is visited by the divine law of retribution which first makes her suffer severe emotional distress and physical pain at the hands of a depraved mob who sexually abuse her. It then condemns her to a shocking death and causes her body to be displayed throughout the land.[92] This instant retribution of a woman's trespass is justified by Biblical exegesis on the grounds that whereas:

---

[86] Genesis 38.15/26
[87] Ibid., 49.8/12
[88] 2 Samuel 11.4
[89] Ibid., 12.13
[90] 90. 1 Chronicles 29.28
[91] Judges 19.2/29
[92] Ibid., 19.25/9

'by the law of Moses, she should have been put to death for her adultery, she escaped the punishment from men, yet vengeance pursued her and God judged her.'[93]

Such divine vengeance does not appear to visit men with whom these women are stated to have played a whore or else who hold them at mercy and abuse them against their will. This bias is shown in favour of men although the Law states quite clearly:

'If a man be found lying with a woman married to another man, then they shall both die, both the man that lay with the woman, and the woman.'[94]

Ironically, exponents of the Biblical law not only justify this singular bias against the female species but also condone the wretched and despicable act of the morally base and degenerate mob who ravish a solitary women in a manner not even the most hardened criminal would want to abuse any woman. They state:

'Though her father had countenanced her, and her husband had forgiven her, and the fault was forgiven now that the quarrel was made up, yet God remembered it against her, when he suffered these wicked men thus wretchedly to abuse her; in doing so which, how unrighteous soever they were, in permitting it the Lord was righteous. The punishment answered her sin, lust was her sin and lust was her punishment.'[95]

---

[93] Henry. Illustrated National Family Bible, p. 282
[94] Deuteronomy 22.22
[95] Henry. Illustrated National Family Bible, p. 282

Yet, while women are instantly made to pay for their men who commit such unrighteous deeds and visit women to satiate their physical lust are not only permitted to condemn to death, the women with whom they commit sin[96] but the law of divine retribution also overlooks their transgression and bestows greater bounty and reward upon them and their posterity.[97] Biblical exegesis once again justify such instant retribution on the grounds:

> 'How just and even is the course which the Almighty Judge holds in all his retribution! This woman had shamed the bed of a Levite by her former wantonness, and had thus far gone away smoothly with her sins. Now, when the world had forgotten her offence, God called her to reckoning, and punished her with her own sin. Adultery was her sin - adultery was her death.'[98]

But men who commit an enormity of a much more serious nature, including incest[99] and also forceful abduction, rape and eventually murder of the ravished victim's lawful husband[100] are able to personally escape divine retribution. In fact, the recompense for their sin is eventually extracted by the Biblical law of divine retribution[101], often from the offender's extremely innocent, pious and righteous female descendants[102] while the offenders themselves are bestowed with divine grace and multiple favours throughout their lives[103] and unto death.[104]

---

[96] Genesis 38.15/24
[97] Ibid., 49.8/12
[98] Hall. Illustrated National Family Bible, p. 283
[99] Genesis 38.15/18
[100] 2 Samuel 11.4/17
[101] Stackhouse. Illustrated National Family Bible, p. 341
[102] 2 Samuel 13.1/21
[103] 1 Chronicles 14.17
[104] 1 Chronicles 29.28

SCRIPTURAL HUMILIATION OF WOMEN

It has already been shown that a man who forcefully violates a woman's chastity and is proven guilty of the offence is able to atone his sin with a token penalty of fifty shekels of silver, paid, not to the victim who has been abused and whose honour dented, but to another man whose property has been violated - the father of the virgin defiled by the offender. This penalty, when looked at from another angle, rather than being a punishment, is a price paid by the offender to permanently purchase the flesh of a female human being - for him to further satiate his physical lust with the full sanction of the Law.

In sharp contrast to this, a Judaeo-Christian woman who is wrongfully accused of adultery by her jealous husband has to suffer physical pain as well as emotional and spiritual humiliation. Biblical ordinances demand that if a husband is overcome with a spirit of jealousy to accuse his wife of adultery and, if in the absence of witnesses against her, he should bring her to a priest, then the priest shall uncover the accused woman's head and pronounce a curse upon her to the effect that 'if she hath gone aside to uncleanliness and lain with another man and if she be defiled' then:

> **'The Lord make thee a curse and an oath among thy people, and make thy thigh to rot, and thy belly to swell.'**[105]

The priest shall then cause her to drink a potion of bitter water that is supposed to put this divine curse into effect. If after all this physical and psychological humiliation, the wife is proven innocent of the charge, she is made to return to her husband's

---

[105] Numbers 5.13/21

house to conceive a seed of and for her jealous spouse as though nothing had happened.[106]

That however, is not the extent of the pain which the innocent wife has to suffer. Although unblemished and chaste, yet Biblical law demands that she bear her iniquity while the jealous male who wrongfully accuses his thoroughly pure and pious wife is considered to be free of guilt. The ordinances of the Judaeo- Christian scriptures state in relation to this:

> **'This is the law of jealousies, when a wife goeth aside to another instead of her husband, and is defiled; Or when the spirit of jealousy cometh upon him, and he be jealous over his wife, and shall set the woman before the Lord, and the priest shall execute upon her all this law. Then shall the man be guiltless from iniquity, and this woman shall bear her iniquity.'[107]**

Although this pure and chaste and innocent and unblemished wife of a jealous husband has not committed any offence, the Law refuses to give her a clean bill of conduct. Instead, it demands that she should bear her iniquity - a judgement which any civilized society would consider a mockery of justice. Yet, despite subjecting the honour of a pious woman to humiliation, the upholders of the Biblical law justify this singular bias against the female species to argue that:

> **'Even when the husband's jealousy was groundless, he would not be accounted guilty if he took this method of cleaning up the matter.'[108]**

---

[106] Ibid., 5.22/8
[107] Ibid., 5.29/31
[108] Scott. Illustrated National Family Bible, p. 148

This kind of an excuse is in itself evidence of male chauvinism fully supported by the injunctions of the Biblical law which permit a jealous husband to falsely accuse an innocent woman of an abominable capital offence; subject her to physical pain and psychological distress; bring disgrace upon her and suffer her public humiliation. And yet, at the end of all this, be considered absolutely free of guilt and thoroughly justified in taking such severe action against an innocent wife on account of mere jealousy.

CRIPTURAL CONTEMPT OF THE FEMALE SPECIES

This manner of bias against women in a Judaeo-Christian society may be an extension of the extreme contempt in which Biblical scriptures have held the female species since the beginning of time. Its first lady, the alleged progenitor of the human race has already been shown to have had no place in God's original design of creation. She is stated to have been an afterthought, created to compliment Yahweh's already planned creation and believed to have been brought into being with only one explicit purpose - to be a help meet for the man whom the Lord had created in His own image and likeness and whom He desired not to leave alone.[109]

But the worst insult which Eve has had to suffer is the Biblical insinuation that she 'was the first human sinner' and therefore, she has to shoulders the responsibility of 'putting mankind out of harmony with its Creator and bringing consequences of enormous evil upon the entire human race.'[110] According to the Biblical version of mankind's fall from grace, Eve enticed her husband Adam into transgression

---

[109] Genesis 2.18/23
[110] Aid to Bible Understanding, Watch Tower Bible Society., p. 1505

after having transgressed herself.[111] It is also alleged that Adam himself accused his wife of being responsible for the sin committed in the garden of Eden. He is reported by events recorded by the Bible to have justified himself in the presence of Yahweh with the submission:

> **'The woman which thou gavest to be with me, she gave me of the tree, and I did eat.'[112]**

While the female species is held responsible for the burden of sin borne by mankind by the Hebrew Pentateuch, one would have thought that Christianity's unique relationship with a woman - Mary, the blessed mother of Christ would have given the Church fathers some reason to lessen this unfortunate insult upon its womenfolk. But Christianity, instead of shouldering responsibility of man's own human failings, shifted the burden of mankind's sin upon the tender shoulders of a woman by alleging that it 'took birth in the heart and mind of a woman who coveted what rightly belonged to Jehovah as her Sovereign and conformed herself to the ways, standards and will of the devil in contradiction to her Creator and also her God appointed head, her husband.'[113] It excuses man's disobedience to the explicit command of the Lord on the pretext that:

> **'Adam was not deceived but the woman, being deceived, was in transgression.'[114]**

Although the Biblical Adam himself is stated to have partaken of the forbidden fruit in the garden of Eden, the Judaeo Christian scriptures insist that it was 'Eve who was beguiled by the serpent.'[115] Adam's responsibility is mitigated with the

---

[111] Genesis 3.1/12
[112] Ibid., 3.12
[113] Aid to Bible Understanding, Watch Tower Bible Society, p. 1505
[114] Timothy 2.14
[115] 2 Corinthians 11.3

41

excuse that the 'man's sin differed from that of his wife in that Adam was not deceived by the tempter's propaganda but Eve, putting trust in the tempter's words, let herself be seduced.'[116] Adam is thus shown as an innocent party who became involved in this transgression due to 'his desire for his wife'[117] who contrived to 'seek happiness from departing from God'[118] and thereby, 'improper desires begun to work in the woman'[119] as a result of which 'she became a transgressor of God's law and then approached her husband and induced him to join her in disobedience to God.'[120] Consequently, 'man damaged his relations, not only with God but also his relations with the rest of God's creation including damage to man's own self, to his mind, his heart and his body.'[121]

Women in the Judaeo Christian cultures have, therefore, suffered great humiliation at the hands of the Church fathers who have traditionally accused her species of being the 'first in transgression' and also, 'who being deceived, brought the man into transgression also.'[122] They appear to have never given a second thought to the contempt which they direct against the female species which includes their mothers and sisters and also wives and daughters. Saint Chrysostom humbled them by stating that they were 'an inevitable evil, an eternal mischief, an attractive calamity and a decorated misfortune' and Gregory the Great called them 'the poison of the asp and the malice of the dragon.' Saint Bonaventure debased them as 'scorpions ever ready to sting' and Saint Jerome denounced them 'as the gate of the devil.' Saint Barnabas branded them as 'the organs of the devil' and Saint

---

[116] Aid to Bible Understanding, Watch Tower Bible Society, p. 1505
[117] Ibid.
[118] Scott. Illustrated National Family Bible, p 1119
[119] Aid to Bible Understanding, Watch Tower Bible Society, p. 1505
[120] Ibid., p. 538
[121] Ibid., p. 1505
[122] Henry. Illustrated National Family Bible, p. 1147

Tertullian belittled them as' beings who opened the door to satanic temptation and corrupted the image of God.'

Sadly, while Adam's actions are justified on the grounds that 'he was persuaded into this transgression by his wife and was overcome by his importunity[123]', Biblical scholars seem reluctant to consider the human limitations of Eve who was beguiled by a force much more powerful than the persuasive power which she, as a mortal being, could have ever exercised. On the contrary, they hold her responsible for her actions and state that she took the forbidden fruit herself which:

> **'was her own act and deed. The devil did not take it, and put it into her mouth, whether she would or no; but she herself took it. Satan may tempt, but he cannot force."[124]**

UNCLEAN OBJECTS OF SEXUAL GRATIFICATION

The Judaeo Christian literature also indicates that women are considered spiritually unclean creatures worthy of being objects of sexual gratification and agents of human procreation only. Although Biblical standards find it permissible and proper for consecrated men to marry certain women and physically cohabit with them, yet, one finds that while they had neither scruples about engaging into holy matrimony with these females nor qualms about having intimate physical liaison with them, they still considered them unworthy to live in consecrated places of holiness and piety. This is indicated in the Bible which states:

---

[123] Ibid. p. 4
[124] Ibid.

43

'Solomon brought up the daughter of Pharaoh out of the city of David unto the house that he hath built for her: for he said, My wife shall not dwell in the house of David king of Israel, because the places are holy, whereunto the ark of the Lord hath come.'125

Apparently, the reason why these lawfully wedded wives, including those of noble blood such as the daughter of the Egyptian Pharaoh whom Solomon married are considered physically worthy of Judaeo Christian men but spiritually unworthy of living in consecrated places may be found in Biblical concepts which find the female species spiritually unclean to the extent that it is considered unable to produce anything pure or righteous - including its male offspring. Hence, it is stated:

'What is man, that he should be clean? and he which is born of a woman, that he should be righteous?'126

On another occasion, Job assumes that man cannot be justified with God because of his inherent impurity in consequence of being born of a woman. He states:

'How then can man be justified with God? or how can he be clean that is born of a woman?'127

Consequently, women have been regarded as being 'necessary indeed and justifiable for the propagation of species'128 but at the same time, a:

---

125 2 Chronicles 8.11
126 Job 15.14
127 Job 25.4
128 Lecky, W.H. History of European Morals

44

'condition of degradation which men who aspire to real sanctity ought to avoid.'[129]

An extreme view indeed! but it appear to be based on certain pronouncements of Christ who admonished his congregation:

'For there are some eunuchs, which are born so from their mother's womb; and there are some eunuchs which are made eunuchs of men; and there be eunuchs, which have made themselves eunuchs for the kingdom of heaven's sake. He that is able to receive it, let him receive it.'[130]

Celibacy has, therefore, been considered a holier state in Christianity while marriage a pollution and sacrilege since Paul not only believed that 'it is good for a man not to touch a woman'[131] but also 'wished that every man was like himself - celibate'[132] Thus, a monastic system has been imposed upon the clergy of the oldest and the largest Christian church although it defies the very purpose for which Yahweh is stated by the Bible to have created a man and a woman, that is, the multiplication of the human race.[133]

CONDEMNED TO LIFE OF PERPETUALSORROW, PAIN AND SUBJUGATION

Yet, while women have been created as an essential instrument to fill the earth, they have been condemned by the Judaeo-Christian scriptures to a life of perpetual sorrow and pain and also subjugation to man on account of God's

---

[129] Ibid.
[130] Matthew 19.12
[131] 1 Corinthians 7.1
[132] Ibid., 7.7
[133] Genesis 1.27/8

alleged curse upon the Biblical Eve for her transgression in the garden of Eden. Apparently, the Lord, wroth with the first lady of the Biblical civilization stated to her:

> **'I shall greatly multiply thy sorrow and thy conception; in sorrow shall thou bring forth children; and thy desire shall be thy husband, and he shall rule over thee.'**[134]

She has, on account of this alleged original curse upon her species, spent her life in sorrow while man has ruled over her ever since. But sadly, it appears that even in punishment, fate has been kinder to men than to women since he, similarly sentenced to a life of sweat and toil for his part of the transgression in the garden of Eden[135] has alleviated his punishment by shifting half the burden of his sentence upon his other half. A woman traditionally toils in affliction to assist her husband and in the sweat of her face she eats bread while she also continues to be ruled by him and bears children in pain without the man being either willing or even able to share her sentence - a sentence which she shall continue to carry for as long as her species exists on earth.

INEQUALITY IN BIRTH

Finally, Biblical scriptures not only show singular bias against women from the onset of creation but unto this day and age with the birth of every female offspring in a Judaeo-Christian culture. A mother, for instance, is considered physically unclean for seven days and spiritually impure for thirty three days after the birth of a male offspring as declared by the Biblical law of purification:

---

[134] Ibid., 3.16
[135] Ibid., 3.19

> 'If a woman have conceived seed, and born a man child: then she shall be unclean for seven days; according to the days of the separation of her infirmity shall she be unclean. And in the eight day the flesh of his foreskin shall be circumcised. And she shall then continue in the blood of her purifying three and thirty days: she shall touch no hallowed thing, nor come into the sanctuary, until the days of her purifying be fulfilled.'[136]

But, on the birth of a female child, the same law doubles this period of uncleanliness and impurity for the Judaeo Christian mother and defines her as physically unclean for a period of fourteen and spiritually impure for a period of sixty days. It states:

> 'But if she bear a maid child, then she shall be unclean two weeks, as in her separation; and she shall continue in the blood of her purifying threescore and six days.'[137]

This bias shown against the birth of a female offspring by the Biblical literature has absolutely no apparent reason whatsoever. There is neither any moral justification for it nor medical grounds and Judaeo-Christian scholars themselves are at a loss to give any acceptable reason as to why this difference observed in Biblical law - except that it is possibly:

> 'in remembrance of the curse upon the woman that was first in transgression.'[138]

This excuse is evidence of the irrationality in the Judaeo Christian teachings, the proponents of which continue to

---

[136] Leviticus 12.2/4
[137] Ibid., 12.5
[138] Henry. Illustrated National Family Bible, p., 118

remain obstinate and not admit a flaw in it. On the contrary, to save themselves the embarrassment, they direct every kind of unpleasantness to the female species and hold it in extreme contempt - irrespective of whether or not it reflects favourably upon their own species. In the course of this humiliation of women, Biblical scholars are even prepared to hold themselves to ridicule by stating:

'This ceremonial uncleanliness which the law laid women in childbed under, was to signify the pollution of sin, which we are all conceived and born in. For if the root is impure, so is the branch: Who can bring a clean thing out of an unclean?'[139]

This is the height of insult one could dispense upon the female species although as an expectant mother, she carries her child's burden within herself for a considerably long period and nourishes the infant to maturity with her untiring concern and constant love. She sacrifices her rest and leisure to her child's comfort and spends sleepless nights to meet one's often overbearing demands. She also remains concerned of the welfare of her offspring throughout her life, even when they are past the age of childhood and continues to worry of them even when her children are parents within their own right.

As a wife, she sacrifices much of her independence and leisure to bring comfort to her family, more often than not, even allowing herself to be reduced to a manual labourer at home. She keeps alert from dawn to dusk and even through the dark nights and neither resents or begrudge the husband's peaceful sleep when her infant or sick children demand her attention at the most unsocial hours. Being a much stronger person emotionally, she often sustains and

---

[139] Ibid.

comforts her spouse in adversity with her sensitive nature, sympathetic disposition and loving concern.

As a sister too, a woman proves to be a pillar of strength to the family while as a daughter, she offers eternal love. Yet, sadly, her status is represented by the early Church fathers in the Judaeo-Christian cultures as that of:

'The door of hell and the mother of all human ills. She should be ashamed at the very thought that she is a woman. She should live in continuous penance on account of the curses she brought upon the world. She should be ashamed of her dress for it is the memorial of her fall. She should be especially ashamed of her beauty for it is the most potent instrument of the demon.'[140]

Apparently, Tertullian, the reputed second century Church father held women responsible for all the ills which befell mankind and also the death of Jesus Christ. Hence he stated:

'Do you know that you are each an Eve? The sentence of God on this sex of yours in this age: the guilt must of necessity live too. You are the devils' gateway; you are the unsealer of that forbidden tree; you are the first deserters of the divine law; you are she who persuades him whom the devil was not valiant enough to attack. You destroyed so easily God's image, man. On account of your desert ~ that is death ~ even the son of God had to die.'[141]

May God preserve mankind against such views and opinions in relation to a species which portrays the best in human nature - as a mother, a wife, a sister or a daughter? Amen!

---

[140] Lecky, W.H. History of European Moral
[141] Ibid.

49

CHAPTER THREE

WOMEN IN ISLAM

The birth of a female offspring in a pre-Islamic household was traditionally a matter of grave concern and often grief in almost all known civilizations and in Arabia itself, women occupied an extremely low position. They were looked upon as mere chattels owned by their menfolk and viewed as objects of sexual gratification or child procreation by the Arabs. It was a custom amongst them to, not only own as many wives or concubines and female slaves as they wished or could afford in a polygamous structure but, with the consent of other males, also share some women as common wives amongst themselves. Consequently, a female in this kind of an arrangement was expected to wife a group a number of husbands. If she conceived a seed and delivered a child, she was required to assemble all her husbands and present the child to whichever of these men she thought was the father.[1]

---

[1] Sahih Bukhari, 62. 37

On the other hand, a woman fortunate enough to be married to one man only could be made to submit to conjugal relations with other men - either to provide her husbands with an heir if her spouse was sterile or else he wished to fulfil a desire of an heir of noble stock. In such situations, Arabian wives found themselves subjected to physical and psychological abuse by strangers until they finally conceived and the signs of their pregnancy were apparent to the naked eye. In the meantime, their lawful husbands normally abstained from any physical contact with them, particularly if the purpose of the exercise was to procure an heir of noble stock.[2]

Besides being denied a right over their own body, females in the Arabian society did not own personal property except in some isolated cases amongst nobility. Nor were they given a right to share the legacy of their parents and husbands or even children. They were, themselves, subject to being inherited as part of property by the sons of their deceased husbands who were at liberty to deal with the wives or concubines of their fathers in whatever manner deemed fit or expedient. The sons could either legally marry their own step mothers or retain them as concubines. These unfortunate widows could also be married to other people by their inheritors or presented as gifts to other men and even disposed off as mere chattels. Those who inherited these females or received them as a gift retained an absolute right to deny them permission to marry a person of their own choice.[3]

That was not the extent of scorn and deprivation to which the female species was subjected in the Arabian society. The Arabs looked upon women with such contempt that they even discriminated against them in matters of food and basic nourishment. It was a custom amongst the Arabian people to reserve a portion of their crop and cattle, a part of which they

---

[2] Ibid.

assigned to God and a part to their deities. They insisted that none could eat of this except whom they pleased[3] and women where the principle species forbidden to partake from what had been reserved by their menfolk as an act of nobility and charity. The Quran refers to this Arabian tradition and states:

> **'They also assert: That which is in the womb of such and such cattle is exclusively for our males and is forbidden to our females; but if it be born dead, they can all share in it.'[4]**

Another abominable offence with which Arabia was burdened with in relation to women was that of infanticide. Female infants were buried alive in the desert and mothers were often made to commit this barbarous deed themselves. In the early years of Islam, it drew the attention of mankind to this deplorable attitude towards the birth of female offspring and stated that the divines and soothsayers and astrologers of the pre-Islamic era:

> **'made the slaying of their children appear pleasing to many of the idolaters that they may ruin them and cause confusion in their religion.'[5]**

It also referred to the emotional turmoil in which a person delivered with a female child found himself and the disgrace which he felt the infant had brought upon him on account of the accepted conventions of the Arabian society. It stated that:

> **'when to one of them is conveyed the tidings of a female child, his face is overcast with gloom and he is deeply agitated. He seeks to hide himself from the people because of the ominous news**

---

[3] Ibid., Kitabul Ikrah, 6
[4] Al Quran 6.137/9
[5] Ibid., 6.140

which he has had. Shall he preserve it despite the disgrace involved or bury it in the ground?'[6]

The Quran warned that people who consider their female offspring a source of shame; whose faces are overcast with gloom on the birth of daughters; who feel deeply agitated when the news of the birth of daughters is conveyed to them; who consider the birth of female offspring a matter of disgrace; who contemplate infanticide of these infants and who finally slay them and bury them are such as have gone away from the path righteousness. It stated:

'Losers indeed are they who slay their children foolishly out of ignorance, and make unlawful that which Allah has provided for them, fabricating a lie against Allah. They have gone astray and have not chosen to be rightly guided.'[7]

RIGHT TO LIFE SECURED

Infanticide was condemned by Islam in no uncertain terms and people who buried their daughters alive were threatened that they shall be called to account for their conduct and misdeeds when God shall gather mankind together and set alight the blazing fire of Hell. The Quran warned that when:

'people are brought together; and when the female infant buried alive is questioned about: For what crime was she killed? And when books are spread abroad, and when the heaven is laid bare, and when hell is stoked up, and when the

---

[6] Ibid., 16.59/60
[7] Ibid., 6.141

> Garden is brought nigh, then everyone will know that which he has wrought.'[8]

Consequently, the evil practice of killing infant children for whatever reason it was perpetrated was proscribed with explicit injunctions which demanded:

> 'slay not your offspring for fear of poverty. It is We who provides for them and for you. Surely, slaying them is a grave sin.'[9]

Abstention from this abominable practice which burdened Arabia in particular and the world in general was made an essential article of Islamic faith and the Prophet of Islam, Muhammad[sa] was commanded by God to announce:

> 'Come, let me rehearse to you what your Lord has enjoined: that you associate not anything as partner with Him; that you behave benevolently towards your parents; that you slay not your offspring. It is We who provide for you and for them.'[10]

A vow to abstain from killing innocent children was made a pre requisite to joining the fold of Islam by Divine injunctions which directed:

> 'O Prophet! when believing women come to thee, offering their allegiance that they will not associate anything with Allah, nor will they steal, neither commit adultery, nor kill their children, or bring false accusation of unchastity nor disobey thee in that which is right, then

---

[8] Ibid., 81.8/15
[9] Ibid., 17.32
[10] Ibid., 6.152

accept their allegiance and ask Allah to forgive them.'[11]

While the Quran defined infanticide as a grievous sin - as grievous as associating partners with the One and Only God[12], Prophet Muhammad[sa] depicted it as an abominable profanity second only to idolatry[13] and one of the seven most destructive and sacrilegious deeds which Muslims ought to abstain from.[14] He also imposed a duty upon every parent to deal equitably with children[15] and declared that a person who did not bury his daughter alive nor humiliate her or give a son preference over her would be admitted into Paradise.[16] Consequently, the female species began to be spared the brutal treatment which was meted upon it since times immemorial and women came to be respected as a distinct and an essential creation of God Almighty - created as a consequence of His pleasure and not as an essential appendage to complement the Lord's already planned creation as in the Bible.[17] The Quran bore testimony to this distinct creation of the female species and stated:

'To Allah belongs the Kingdom of the heavens and the earth. He creates what He pleases. He bestows females upon whom He pleases and He bestows males upon whom He pleases, or, He grants them both, males and females; and He makes whom He pleases barren. Surely, He is All Knowing, Determiner of the measure.'[18]

---

[11] Ibid., 60.13
[12] Ibid., 6.152
[13] Sahih Muslim 1.38
[14] Sahih Bukhari 82.31
[15] Sahih Muslim 10.644
[16] Masnad Ahmad
[17] Genesis 2.18
[18] Al Quran 42.50/1

55

EQUALITY IN CREATION

Islam is thus the first religion which secures women a Divine right to live as a blessed creation of God while assigning to them their rightful place in Allah's original design. It acknowledges an independent creation of the female species from the very beginning of creation and states:

'O mankind, be mindful of your duty to your Lord, Who created you from a single soul and of its kind created its mate: and from them twain spread many men and women.'[19]

The Biblical concept that a woman was fashioned out of a man's rib[20] is thoroughly rejected in Islamic thought which stresses upon the distinct identity of the female species from the onset of creation. It states:

'He it is Who created you from a single soul and of the same did He make its mate.'[21]

On yet another occasion, the Quran refers to the creation of mankind - both, the male and the female species and declares:

'O ye people! fear your Lord Who created you from a single being; then of the same kind its mate.'[22]

It also refutes the Biblical concept that a woman was created to be a helper for a man in the sense that she was created for him and not he for her[23] and declares that God created a

---

[19] Al Quran 4.2
[20] Genesis 2.21/2
[21] Al Quran 7.190
[22] Ibid., 39.7
[23] 1 Corinthians 11.9

woman for a man as much as He created a man for a woman. It states:

> **'Of His Signs is that He has created spouses for you of your own kind so that you may find peace of mind through them, and He has put love and tenderness between them.'**[24]

Furthermore, whereas the Biblical woman is stated to have been created for the need of the man to serve him in subjection in everything[25], Islam maintains that the two species have been made interdependent upon each other and none amongst them claims greater importance in God Almighty's ultimate design of creation. Consequently, it admonishes men that women:

> **'are garments for you while you are garments for them.'**[26]

The Quran also assigns an equitable position to the female species in its relationship with its male counterpart and denies the Biblical concept of male superiority and lordship. It states that:

> **'The believers, men and women are friends of one another.'**[27]

Moreover, while a Biblical woman has been condemned to a life of perpetual desire of her husband from the onset of creation - a husband who is to rule her in subjection[28], Islam removes this curse thrust upon the female species by the Judaeo Christian scriptures. It declares that the creation of

---

[24] Al Quran 30.22
[25] Ephesians 5.22/4
[26] Al Quran 2.188
[27] Ibid., 9.71
[28] Genesis 3.16

spouses, male and female from amongst themselves is a Sign bestowed upon mankind so that it:

'may find peace of mind through them and He has put love and tenderness between them. In that surely are Signs for a people who reflect.'[29]

Hence, in Islamic thought, the female species has been acknowledged a distinct and an independent creation of God from the onset of creation and assigned a place on the par with its male counterpart.

SPIRITUAL EQUALITY AND INDEPENDENCE

Since Islam admits the position of the female species as a distinct and independent creation from the onset of creation, it establishes the spiritual equality and independence of women on the par with their male counterparts. It assigns to them absolute freedom to pursue their spiritual goals and bestows upon them complete independence in matters pertaining to their spiritual welfare. They are free to engage in exercises of spiritual advancement without either being restricted or else being dependent upon the pleasure of their menfolk, whether these be their fathers or husbands and the Quran guarantees the righteous among them similar spiritual blessings of purity as it pledges to righteous men in an Islamic congregation. It declares that:

'Of the believers whoso acts righteously, whether male or female, We will surely grant such a one pure life; and We will certainly reward them according to the measure of the best of their works.'[30]

---

[29] Al Quran 30.22
[30] Ibid., 16.98

It promises women that they shall not be deprived of the mercy of God but that they shall be as much recipients of it as their menfolk:

> 'The consequence of responsibility under the Law is that Allah will punish the hypocrites, men and women, and the idolaters, men and women; and Allah will turn in mercy to the believers, men and women. Allah is Most Forgiving, Ever Merciful.'[31]

God Almighty also declares in the Quran that men and women are spiritually related and similar in character and promises that He shall not cause the spiritual labour and righteous deeds of anyone, whether of the male or the female species, to be lost. He states:

> 'I will not suffer the labours of any labourer from among you, male or female, to perish. You are spiritually akin to one another.'[32]

He also declares that those people, whether male or female, who suffer in His cause shall have their ills removed from them and they shall be bestowed the best of rewards. He promises in the Quran:

> 'I will surely remove their ills and I will admit them to Gardens through which streams flow - a reward from Allah, with Allah is the best of rewards.'[33]

This reward promised to the righteous amongst God's creation is not subject to the redeeming or sacrificial blood of any single male as in Christian philosophy according to which,

---

[31] Ibid., 33.74
[32] Ibid., 3.196
[33] 34. Ibid.

it was God's 'good pleasure for all the fullness to dwell in Jesus and through him, to reconcile all things to Himself, having made peace through the blood of Christ.'[34] It is offered independently to the entire human race, irrespective of the recipient's age, creed or sex as clearly evident from the Quranic passage:

> 'For men who submit themselves wholly to Allah and women who submit themselves wholly to Him, and men who believe and women who believe, and men who are obedient and women who are obedient, and men who are truthful and women who are truthful, and men who are steadfast and women who are steadfast, and men who are humble and women who are humble, and men who give alms and women who give alms, and men who fast and women who fast, and men who guard their chastity and women who guard their chastity, and men who remember Allah women who remember Him - Allah has prepared forgiveness and a great reward.'[35]

The pleasure of God which according to Islamic thought is the ultimate reward to which mankind can aspire is promised to the female species as much as it is promised to its male counterparts:

> Allah has promised the believers, men and women, Gardens beneath which rivers flow, wherein they will abide, and delightful dwelling places in Gardens of Eternity, and the pleasure

---

[34] Colossians 1.19/20
[35] Al Quran 33.36

of Allah, which is the greatest bounty of all. That is the supreme triumph.'[36]

The Quran states that God has bestowed upon women the capacity to increase their faith and thereby earn this supreme triumph and be admitted to the Gardens of Paradise:

'He it is Who has sent down tranquillity upon the hearts of the believers that they might add to their faith - to Allah belongs the hosts of the heavens and the earth, and Allah is All Knowing, Wise - that He may admit the believers, men and women, into the Gardens beneath which rivers flow, wherein they will abide, and that He may remove their ills from them - that in the sight of Allah is a supreme triumph.'[37]

It also declares that men and women shall be equally rewarded according to their deeds irrespective of their gender:

'Of the believers whoso acts righteously, whether male of female, We will surely grant such a one a pure life; and We will certainly reward them according to the measure of the best of their works.'[38]

Women are also promised that they shall not be wronged as much as a little hollow in the back of a date stone but that the righteous amongst them shall enter Paradise wherein they will be provided without measure:

---

[36] Ibid., 9.72
[37] Ibid., 48.5/6
[38] Ibid., 16.98

> **'Whoso does good works, whether male or**
> **female, and is a believer, such shall enter**
> **Paradise, and shall not be wronged a whit.'[39]**

This promise is often repeated by the Quran which does not discriminate between a male and a female's right to spiritual rewards. It states on another occasion:

> **'Whoso does good, whether male or female, and**
> **is a believer, these will enter the Garden; they**
> **will be provided therein without measure.'[40]**

Islam does not subscribe to the naive dogma that women shall be redeemed and forgiven of their sins as an act of grace on account of a God's pleasure in a single male - a dogma which forms the essential creed of Christian belief and insists that forgiveness of sins and redemption rests in Christ.[41] The Quran assures women that they shall enter Paradise as a consequence of their own faith in Allah and their personal act of submission to His will. It also guarantees them that they shall enjoy all the delights of Paradise to which they have been made heirs on account of their personal conduct in their lives:

> **'O My servants, there is no fear for you this day,**
> **nor shall you grieve; You who believed in Our**
> **signs and submitted. Enter the Garden, you and**
> **your companions, delighted and joyful. Dishes**
> **and cups of gold will be passed round to them,**
> **and in them will be all that the hearts desire and**
> **in which the eyes delight. Therein will you abide.**
> **This is the Garden to which you have been made**
> **heirs, because of that which you practised.**

---

[39] Ibid., 4.125
[40] Ibid., 40.41
[41] Colossians 1.13/14

Therein for you is fruit in abundance of which you will eat.[142]

In view of this spiritual equality bestowed upon the female species, women are free to pursue their spiritual goals without being dependent upon the pleasure of their fathers or husbands as Biblical women are found to be dependent in Judaism which restricts daughters and wives the right to fulfil their spiritual obligations if forbidden by her fathers or husbands[43] and also in Christianity which binds women to their menfolk by the Law.[44] On the contrary, Islam demands of its men that they neither restrain their womenfolk from engaging in pursuits of spiritual advancement nor restrict them from their duty to their Lord and to gladly allow them to fulfil their religious obligations.[45] Even if, to accomplish this, women have to go to the mosques at nights.[46] This right, Muslim men of faith and integrity have respected throughout the history of Islam and Muslim women of piety and devoutness have exercised without fear of recrimination by their menfolk.[47] Hadeeth literature records that Umar ibn Khattab[ra], the second Caliph did not take kindly to his wife visiting the mosque to offer congregational prayers at night. When she was once asked why she came to the mosque at that time of the night when her husband disliked it, she enquired as to what prevented him from stopping her. She was told that the statement of Allah's Apostle[sa] - 'Do not stop Allah's women slaves from going to Allah's mosques' prevented him.[48] In fact, women in Islam have also been given absolute freedom to disobey their husbands in sinful matters even if ordered by them and such permission forms

---

[42] Al Quran 43.69/74
[43] Numbers 30.3/8
[44] Romans 7.1/2
[45] Sahih Bukhari 62.117
[46] Ibid. 13.11
[47] Ibid.
[48] Ibid.

an integral part of the Islamic Law.[49] This right is unique to Muslim women only and there is not even a comparative parallel to it in any other religion of the world.

SPIRITUAL PERFECTION OF WOMEN

Islam not only recognises the spiritual independence and equality of the female species and its capacity to acquire extremely high standards of spiritual sublimity, but also acknowledges the spiritual perfection of women in no lesser terms than that of their male counterparts. It demonstrates practically, the height of spiritual excellence to which women have risen in their lives as a result of their own personal piety and conduct and bears evidence that they have established such personal contact with their Lord and Creator whereby they have become recipients of the ultimate Divine blessing ever bestowed upon a mortal being within one's life - the blessing of Divine communication and revelation.

According to the Quran, the mother of the great Israelite law giver, Prophet Moses[as], is counted amongst the righteous who excelled to such high standards of spiritual perfection and excellence that she enjoyed communication with her Lord and Master. It is stated that when her suckling infant was threatened by Pharaoh, God Almighty blessed her with the Divine revelation:

> **'Suckle him; and when thou fearest for his life cast him afloat into the river and fear not nor grieve; for We shall restore him to thee and shall make him a Messenger.'[50]**

---

49 Ibid., 62.95
50 Al Quran 28.8

The spiritual excellence to which Jochebed[ra] excelled in her life is not an isolated instance in Islamic history. The virgin Mary[ra], mother of Jesus[as], alleged by Christianity to have inherited the immortal sin committed in the garden of Eden by the first couple and denounced as being herself imperfect and sinful by Christian thought[51] has been raised to an envious height of spiritual perfection and excellence by the Quran. According to its testimony, the blessed Mary[ra] did not require the sacrifice nor the redeeming blood of any man, including her son Jesus[as] to reconcile her to her Creator as assumed in Christian dogma. On the contrary, she was chosen and purified through an independent and direct grace of her Lord and Master - Allah. The Quran states in relation to this:

'Call to mind when the angels said to Mary: Allah has exalted thee and purified thee and chosen thee from among all the women of thy time.'[52]

Islam has acknowledged the spiritual perfection and excellence of women to such high standards that Allah has sets forth as example for those who believe, not men but two women - Assiya[ra], the wife of Pharaoh and Mary[ra], mother of Jesus[as] both of whom were women of unique faith and high spiritual perfection and purity. Hence, the Quran states:

'Allah cites as examples of believers the wife of Pharaoh who prayed: Lord, build for me a house near Thee in the Garden; and deliver me from Pharaoh and his work, and deliver me from the wrongdoing people; and Mary, the daughter of Imran, who guarded her chastity and We sent

---

[51] Aid to Bible Understanding, Watch Tower Bible Society, p. 920
[52] Al Quran 3.43

> **Our Word to her, and she fulfilled the words of her Lord and His Books and was one of the obedient.'[53]**

This excellent spiritual station to which women have been raised in Islam does not have a parallel in any other religion known to mankind . In fact, it is undeniably the only religion which admits the feasibility of women rising to such incredible heights of spiritual perfection and also excels women to this admirable and awe inspiring status.

EVE'S SINGULAR RESPONSIBILITY DENIED

One of the greatest benefits which Islam bestowed upon the entire female species is its categoric denial of a woman's singular responsibility for the breach of covenant in the garden of Eden and its vindication of Eve[as] against the gross charges of having committed the first immortal sin[54] and, thereby being the first human sinner[55] and transgressor of God's law[56] who induced her husband to join her in her disobedience.[57] Paul of Cyrus on whose philosophy modern Christened is based was so insistent that a woman alone bore the responsibility of this transgression which allegedly put mankind out of harmony with its God[58] that he declared:

> **'It was not Adam who was deceived, but the woman being quite deceived fell into transgression.'[59]**

---

[53] Ibid., 66.12/13
[54] Genesis 3.6/17
[55] Aid to Bible Understanding. Watch Tower Bible Soc. p. 1505
[56] Ibid., p. 538
[57] Ibid.
[58] Aid to Bible Understanding. Watch Tower Bible Soc. p. 1505
[59] 1 Timothy 2.14

But, Islam does not subscribe to the Biblical view that Satan first tempted Eve[as] and she in turn lured her husband[60] to make him an involuntary accomplice in her transgression which allegedly brought consequences of great evil upon the entire human race[61] - consequences which to this day mankind suffers in so much that it eats its bread in affliction; it bears children in pain and eventually it suffers death to return to the ground from whence it came, to become dust.[62] Nor does it subscribe to the Judaeo Christian view that the first immortal sin had taken birth in the heart and mind of a woman who let herself be seduced by the serpent.[63]

On the contrary, according to Islamic thought, the accursed Satan did not approach Eve[as] alone but it tempted both Adam[as] and Eve[as] at the same time. The Quran states in relation to this:

'Satan tempted them so that he might make known to them that which was hidden from them of their shame.'[64]

This vindication of Eve[as] singular responsibility is recorded by the Quran elsewhere also, as for instance in the Quranic passage wherein it is stated:

'But Satan caused them both to slip from it, and caused them to depart from the state in which they were.'[65]

The first lady of our post historic civilization and, therefore, the entire female species is exculpated by the Islamic scriptures from singular responsibility of being tempted by the

---

[60] Genesis 3.1/6   62.
[61] Aid to Bible Understanding. Watch Tower Bible Soc, p. 1505
[62] Genesis 3.16/19
[63] Aid to Bible Understanding. Watch Tower Bible Soc, p. 1505
[64] Al Quran 7.21
[65] Ibid., 2.37

devil and of bringing about mankind's fall from grace. That Quran insists that Satan:

> **'swore to them both: Surely I am your sincere counsellor. Thus he brought about their fall by deceit.'[66]**

Incidentally, unlike the Biblical Adam who washed his hands of his responsibility for having disobeyed Yahweh with the excuse that the 'woman whom Thou gavest to be with me, she gave me the tree, and I did eat,'[67] the Quranic Adam[as] never blamed his fault to his wife. The Quran states that when asked for an explanation, both replied:

> **'Our Lord! we have wronged ourselves, and if Thou forgive us not and have not mercy upon us, we shall surely be of the losers.'[68]**

Secondly, Islam does not subscribe to the Pauline concept of immortal sin nor does it lend support to the naive belief that a sin was committed in the garden of Eden by the first couple of our post historic civilization. On the contrary, it maintains that neither Eve[as] nor Adam[as] had any intent to disobey the command of their Lord as evident from the following Quranic passage:

> **'Verily, We had made a covenant with Adam beforehand, but he forgot and We found in him no resolve to disobey.'[69]**

The Quran also states that the blessed couple were led into an unfortunate breach of covenant through deception by the evil Satan who 'brought about their fall by deceit.'[70]

---

[66] Ibid., 7.22/3
[67] Genesis 3.12
[68] Al Quran 7. 24
[69] Ibid., 20.116
[70] Ibid., 7.23

These passages are a clear indication of the fact that the lapse of both, Adam[as] and Eve[as] was an error of judgement and not a deliberate act of disobedience and consequently, the breach of covenant in the garden at Eden being unintentional, Adam[as] and Eve's[as] unfortunate act does not constitute a sin in Islam which draws a clear line between fault and a sin[71], a sin being an intentional act against the will of God while a fault is committed a result of neglect of duty and not rebellion. Hence, the first lady of the post historic human civilization and, allegedly the first Judaeo Christian sinner is exonerated from committing the first sin by Islamic thought. This vindication of a woman pronounces the innocence of the female species and acquits the entire species from the naive Biblical insinuation that of the woman came the beginning of sin which brought consequences of enormous evil upon mankind.

EQUITABLE TREATMENT UNDER LAW

It has already been shown that Biblical ordinances on tort and offenses against persons appear to be sufficiently strict and penalties for transgression excessively harsh. Yet, the Judaeo- Christian scriptures display a singular bias against the female species. For instance, it has been seen that a man who forcefully defiles a chaste and a pious virgin not married or betrothed to another is able to atone his sin and transgression with a token penalty of fifty shekels of silver paid to the victim's father. This, despite the fact that a violent sexual offence with intent has been committed and an innocent woman has been subjected to severe physical pain and humiliation and acute emotional distress.[72]

---

[71] Ibid., 4.113
[72] Deuteronomy 22.28/29

In sharp contrast to this, an unmarried woman who is defiled by a man before she is married and, is then found not to be a virgin is condemned to death by Biblical law which maintains total silence in relation to the male culprit who in the first place defiled her while she was still a virgin.[73] The Judaeo Christian law also overlooks the fact that it may have been quite possible that the lady condemned to death by its injunctions may not have played a whore in her father's home. She may have been an unwilling party in losing her virginity in so much that she could have been raped by her assailant but the traumatic experience of the physical attack by a stranger; the fear of subjecting her parents to emotional distress; the anger of the often hypocritical society at large; the consideration of her personal honour and the reputation of her family and several other such factors may have been instrumental in her being induced to observe silence - a silence which appears to cost the victim her life since the Law makes no provision to trace the male involved in this sacrilege and thereby, possibly establish the innocence of the woman condemned to death. It also shows bias against the female species in so much that while the woman is instantly condemned to death for allegedly playing a whore in her father's house, the male culprit responsible for the defloration of the virgin, whether with or without her consent remains free to lead his life in relative security and possibly indulge in further acts of sinful engagement.

It has also been shown that Biblical convention permits a husband to mercilessly butcher his unfortunate wife, forcefully defiled by a depraved mob, not for any fault of her own but for the cowardice of her guardian or protector - her husband and her host. The male who in the hour of danger determines to sacrifice his wife to a mob and exposes her to fiends[74] by throwing her to their mercy also reserves the right

_____

[73] Ibid., 22.13/21
[74] Bush. Illustrated National Family Bible, p. 283

to be the innocent victim's executioner - to cut her into twelve pieces, limb by limb and send her mutilated body throughout the territory for public display.[75] In this situation also, the Law does not impose a responsibility over him to follow his wife and save her for fear of his own security.[76] The fate suffered by such unfortunate women is attributed to the law of divine retribution which allegedly visits them for their former wantonness[77] and uncleanliness even after their husbands have forgiven and the society at large has forgotten their previous indiscretion.[78]

Yet, this law of divine retribution does not visit men who commit a breach of much more serious nature - as serious as wilful incest with widows of their deceased sons[79] or forceful abduction and rape of women married to other men and, thereafter, wilful murder of the female victim's lawful husbands.[80] These men are able to atone their sins with mere confession of transgression[81] and are not only readily pardoned for this serious breach of the moral code[82] but are endowed with multiple divine blessings throughout their lives so much so that the Lord puts the fear of them into all nations[83] and they die in fullness of age, in riches and honour.[84] They are also able to pass these blessings to their future generations as an act of divine grace.[85] This singular bias in favour of men suggests that the Biblical law of divine retribution itself shows prejudice against the female species since men who violate women are either permitted to stay anonymous or are rewarded for their misdeeds and even

---

[75] Judges 19.25/30
[76] Henry. Illustrated National Family Bible, p. 282
[77] Hall. Ibid
[78] . Henry. Ibid.
[79] Genesis 38.14/18
[80] 2 Samuel 11.4/26
[81] Genesis 38.26
[82] 2 Samuel 12.13
[83] 1 Chronicles 14.17
[84] Ibid., 29.28
[85] Genesis 49.8/12

forgiven and pardoned while women are either condemned to death[86] or presented to their assailants[87] or else visited by instant divine retribution.[88]

Islam removes this blatant injustice in its penal code and treats male and female offenders with equity and justice. In the first instance, it demands that offenders accused of immoral conduct short of adultery be punished equally:

> **'Confront those of your women who are guilty of unbecoming conduct with four witnesses, If they bear witness, then confine the women to their houses till death overtakes them or Allah opens a way for them. And as for the two of you who are guilty thereof, punish them both but if they should repent and amend, then leave them alone. Surely, Allah is Oft- Returning with compassion and Ever Merciful.'[89]**

In cases of a more serious nature also, such as adultery, male and female offenders are treated with equality and the female species does not bear the brunt of the punishment alone. The Quran states in relation to the punishment of adultery:

> **'Flog the adulteress and the adulterer, each one of them, with a hundred stripes, and let not pity for them restrain you from executing the judgement of Allah, if you believe in Allah and the Last Day. Let a party of believers witness their punishment. An adulterer does not consort except with an adulteress or an idolatrous woman, and an adulteress does not consort**

---

[86] Deuteronomy 22.13/23
[87] Ibid., 22.28/9
[88] Judges 19.1/19
[89] Al Quran 4.16/17

**except with an adulterer or an idolatrous man.
Such conduct is forbidden to believers.'[90]**

Islam does not favour either sex in the punishment prescribed for an offence committed in its society and, therefore, men and women, whether married or single are punished equally for their offence.[91] Yet, the penal code of Islam takes into account various factors before it inflicts punishment upon women for their transgression. As for instance, a woman accused and convicted of adultery has her sentence deferred if she is either pregnant or recently delivered of her burden. She is permitted to deliver her child in safety and Islamic law refrains the society from inflicting any kind of punishment on her at least until she has been delivered of her burden and the child has been weaned.[92]

Although Islamic law also stipulates that a male guilty of adultery be sentenced on the basis of his own confession and admission of sin[93], yet the woman implicated in any such allegation does not automatically become a recipient of punishment. She reserves the right to either admit her guilt or deny the allegation and unless she is proven guilty or else she herself confesses her sin, she is not liable to punishment on the basis of the man's admission of unlawful association with her.[94]

Islamic law also inclines more in favour of a woman's denial of a charge of adultery and fornication against her than of a man's allegation[95] if the charge is not proven or substantiated with four witnesses.[96] Even if, at some later stage, the man's allegations against her are proven to have been correct[97], the

---

[90] Ibid., 24.3/4
[91] Sahih Muslim 15.680
[92] Ibid., 15.682
[93] . Sahih Bukhari 82.15
[94] . Ibid., 82.25
[95] Al Quran 24.7/10
[96] Sahih Bukhari 60.210
[97] Ibid., 82.30

entire matter is allowed to rest and no further action is taken against the woman.[98]

ALLEGATIONS OF IMPROPRIETY

Biblical scriptures have been shown to subject a woman wrongfully accused of adultery by her jealous husband to physical pain as well as emotional humiliation. The Judaeo Christian law gives a jealous husband the right to bring his chaste and pious wife to the priest and accuse her of adultery in the absence of evidence or witnesses and an innocent wife, so accused on account of her husband's mere jealousy has to go through a severe physical test prescribed by the Law as well as swear her innocent and call the curse of the Lord Yahweh upon herself if she is lying. Even after she is proven innocent of the groundless charge brought against her, she is made to return to her jealous husband to conceive a seed for and of him despite the fact that in his jealousy, the husband caused her to be subjected her to severe physical pain and emotional distress; cast a slur on her impeccable character and also insulted her piety and humiliated her in public.

The Biblical law also considers this husband who brings a false charges against his chaste wife free of guilt despite the false nature of the allegation. It neither requires him to apologise to her for subjecting her to this unnecessary exercise nor does it expect him to show remorse for his action or else repent and make amends. In the meantime, the innocent woman who has already been subjected to severe physical pain and psychological distress is made to bear iniquity even though she is proven innocent of the charge and has absolutely no cause whatsoever to bear any kind of guilt.[99]

---

[98] Ibid., 60.210
[99] Numbers 5.14/31

Islam views such charges of impropriety brought against women with grave concern and often severe contempt, particularly when the allegations are not substantiated nor supported with witnesses. It considers this offence of falsely accusing women as one of the seven most destructive sins[100] and not only does it punish the culprits but also turns them into social lepers whose evidence is not to be accepted until they show remorse and repent and also make amends. The Quran states in relation to this:

> 'Those who calumniate chaste women but bring
> not four witnesses - flog them with eighty
> stripes, and do not admit their evidence ever
> after, for it is they that are transgressors, except
> those who repent and make amends, for truly
> Allah is Most Forgiving, Merciful.'[101]

Islam also warns mankind against the impropriety of accusing chaste and pious woman and states that their indiscretion is not only punishable in this world with eighty lashes prescribed by Law but it shall occasion great chastisement for them in the world hereafter:

> 'Those who calumniate chaste, unwary and
> believing women are cursed in this world and
> the Hereafter; and for them is a grievous
> chastisement on the day when their tongues and
> their hands and their feet will bear witness
> against them as to that which they used to do.
> On that day Allah will pay them their full
> due.'[102]

The Quran also cautions Muslims against indulgence in the character assassination of women. While it promises greater

---

[100] Sahih Bukhari 82.31
[101] Al Quran 24.5/6
[102] 103. Ibid., 24.24/6

reward to the innocent victims whose character has been subjected to malicious abuse and whose purity and piety has been held in question by the indiscretion of their menfolk, it denounces the slanderers as people who possess evil characteristics and are inclined towards evil things:

> 'Evil things are the characteristics of evil people and evil people are inclined towards evil things; and good things are characteristics of good people and good people are inclined towards good things; these are innocent of what the calumniators allege. For them is forgiveness and an honourable provision.'[103]

It imposes a serious responsibility over a husband who brings a charge of improper conduct and adultery against his wife in the absence of witnesses and demands that he declare his accusation on oath four times and on the fifth, he call the wrath of God Almighty upon himself if he is telling a lie. This requirement is embodied in the injunctions of the Quran which demands that:

> 'In case of those who charge their wives with adultery and have no witnesses thereof except themselves - the evidence of such a one will suffice, if he bears witness four times in the name of Allah that he is telling the truth, and a fifth time that Allah's curse be upon him if he lies.'[104]

Yet, a husband's willingness to accuse his wife of improper conduct; proceed with the oath and also call the wrath of God upon himself does not automatically establish the charge brought by him against his wife. A wife accused of this serious offence by her husband in the absence of witnesses has a

---

[103] Ibid., 24.27
[104] Ibid., 24.7/8

similar right to deny his allegation on oath[105] - an oath which stands far superior to that of her husband since the Quran accepts the wife's plea of innocence as against her husband's accusation of guilt. It states that in such cases where a husband brings a charge of adultery against his wife and takes the oath accusing her of the sin in the absence of witnesses:

> 'the punishment shall be averted from her, if she
> bears witness four times in the name of Allah
> that he has lied, and a fifth time that the wrath
> of Allah be upon her if he has spoken the truth.
> Were it not for Allah's grace and His mercy upon
> you, and that Allah is Compassionate and Wise,
> would have come to grief.'[106]

Islam demands substanive proof from the husband who accuses his wife of the serious charge of adultery[107] and a husband who fails to substantiate his allegation may expect to be punished by law and receive eighty lashes for having brought forth a charge which he cannot prove.[108] If the allegation has to be settled on oath, Islamic Law does not subject the wife to the kind of humiliation meted upon her Judaeo Christian counterpart.[109] Instead, it gives her an opportunity to deny the charge brought against her and plead her innocence on oath[110] which carries more weight than the husband's.[111] A wife so accused by her husband is also spared the agony of having to return to her husband to conceive a seed of and for him as a Judaeo Christian wife is made to return to her jealous husband. Since Islam accepts that a

---

[105] Sahih Bukhari 60.210
[106] Al Quran 24.9/11
[107] Sahih Bukhari 48.22
[108] Al Quran 24.5
[109] Numbers 5.14/31
[110] Sahih Bukhari 63.29
[111] Al Quran 24.7/10

marriage which has been subjected to such suspicion must be inevitably strained and the prospects of the couple being able to live in harmony thoroughly diminished, it permits the accused but exonerated wife an honourable divorce and the couple are allowed to go their separate ways.[112] The matter is then brought to rest even, if at some later stage there are grounds to believe that the wife may have taken a false oath and the husband may have been correct in his allegation against her.[113]

In cases which finally end in divorce, the husband is not entitled to demand from her, the return of any financial settlement that may have been engaged into at the time of the wedding[114] nor any gifts that may have been bestowed upon the spouse by him during the period of the couple's marriage.[115] Islam maintains that if the husband's allegations against his wife be true, then he has already received benefit in so much that the marriage has been consummated but if the charges brought against her are untrue than he had no right to demand anything.[116] Furthermore, if a wife is found pregnant with a child when accused of adultery by her husband, she reserves an exclusive right to the child's custody[117] and she also retains her right to inherit from her offspring's property.[118]

Since the penal code of Islam is based upon a principle that the accused should be given the benefit of doubt in the absence of conclusive proof and that punishment should be avoided as far as possible, even where there is a verbal confession of the offence[119], in situations where husbands

---

[112] Sahih Bukhari 63.27
[113] Ibid., 63.30
[114] Ibid., 63.32
[115] Ibid., 63.33
[116] Ibid. 63.32/33
[117] Ibid., 63.35
[118] Ibid., 63.30
[119] Sahih Muslim 15.682

suspect paternity of children born of their wives on account of the complexion or other physical traits of the children, Islam gives women the benefit of doubt and attempts to remove suspicion on their character and conduct by explaining these traits to the laws of genetics.[120]

Finally, Islam does not restrict its demand that women not be falsely accused of improper conduct and adultery to free women in its society only but it also considers it a grave sin for men to falsely accuse female slaves of improper conduct and illicit sexual activity.[121] It is, therefore, the only religion which respects and protects the honour of the female species, irrespective of their status in life or position in the society.

These rights bestowed upon women in Islam and the zeal with which its Law protects them indicates that the female species has not only been given equitable rights, but to a certain extent, Islamic laws appear to favour women who happen to enjoy a unique position not known to their counterparts in any other religion or culture before or after the advent of Islam. Incidentally, when these unique rights granted to the female species by the Islamic scriptures and convention are considered in the light of their lot in the pre-Islamic era and also the treatment that was being generally meted upon women by their menfolk particularly in Arabia, one cannot but compliment Islam for not only showing consideration towards the female species but also bringing about such a revolution in the status and position of women as was neither known nor is now known to any other religion or civilization. It is the first religion which demolished the taboos attached to the birth of female offspring and secured them a divine right to live as a blessed creation of God Almighty; acknowledged the creation of the female species as a pre destined creation of Lord and recognised its distinct and

---

[120] Sahih Bukhari 63.26
[121] Ibid. 46.21

independent creation from the very beginning; admitted its equality in creation on the par with its male counterpart and rejected the ancient convention of male superiority and lordship; bestowed spiritual independence upon the entire species to engage in the discipline of spiritual refinement and conceded the potential and capacity of women to achieve incredible spiritual refinement; demonstrated the height of spiritual perfection and excellence to which they have risen and set forth their example for mankind to follow; exonerated the species from the gross charge of committing the first immortal sin and pronounced it thoroughly innocent and also bestowed equitable treatment upon women in reward and punishment in this world as well as the world hereafter. With such a track record one has to but admit that Islam is the first and the only religion which effectively liberated the female species from the physical, psychological and spiritual bondage to which it had become accustomed in its history. It is, therefore, not a wonder that in one of the reports recorded in Hadeeth literature, the noble Prophet of Islam, Muhammad[sa] defined virtuous women as:

'The most precious of all the treasures of the world.'[122]

---

[122] Masnad Ahmad

CHAPTER FOUR

SECULAR RIGHTS OF MUSLIM WOMEN

Women in the pre-Islamic civilizations have been shown to have suffered singular bias and severe discrimination in every sphere of their spiritual life. They were denied a place in God Almighty's original design of creation and considered an essential appendage to compliment His Divine plan; stated to have been dependent upon their menfolk for their very existence and, for all practical purposes, born in subjugation to them; considered mere chattel owned by men, for them to deal with as found expedient; believed to be incapable of attaining any kind of spiritual perfection and excellence and denied an independent right to spiritual exercise and also branded as inferior human beings, not subject to equitable rights under human penal laws nor for that matter, the Divine punitive code.

Islam emancipated the female species and delivered it from the spiritual and psychological bondage to which it had become accustomed. It granted women an independent place in God's original plan of creation and assigned to them an equitable place in Allah's original design; acknowledged their distinct entity, interdependent upon their menfolk to a similar degree; recognised their potential to acquire infinite spiritual perfection and removed every form of spiritual discrimination against the species, for them to pursue their independent spiritual goals to a similar degree as their menfolk and also granted them equitable rights in its penal code of offences against morality.

As against the Biblical scriptures, Islam also vindicated the female species from the gross charges of being the mother of sin and placed the responsibility of the initial breach on the shoulders of both, men and women equally.

SECULAR INDEPENDENCE

Every credible religion before the advent of Islam denied its womenfolk an independent right to own personal property. In the Judaeo-Christian culture, a woman remains the property of her father until given in marriage and he retains an absolute right to acquire monetary or material benefit out of his daughter's marriage[1] which cannot be contracted until the bride price has been paid to him.[2] This custom of extracting a bride price out of the prospective bridegroom is not only acceptable to Judaic convention but the Mosaic law itself recognises a father's right to benefit from his daughter's marriage[3] which if not paid in monetary currency can by

---

[1] Genesis 34.11/12
[2] Ibid., 29.18/21
[3] Exodus 22.16

convention be rendered in services[4] or extracted in form of other brutal acts of murder and mutilation of human beings.[5]

The exclusively Christian scriptures which are in essence an extension of the Mosaic law remain silent on this question of bride price. Nonetheless, Christian scholars justify a father's right to benefit from the marriage of his daughter. They state that it serves:

> **'as compensation for the loss of services of the daughter and for the trouble and expense that the parents had undergone in caring for her and educating her.'[6]**

Islam on the other hand not only acknowledges the independent status of children, whether male or female, in a manner not previously known to any other civilization, but it revolutionises the whole sphere of rights bestowed upon them. The Quran states in relation to them:

> **'wealth and children are an ornament of the life of this world; then of these that is converted into a source of permanent beneficence is best in the sight of thy Lord, both in respect of immediate reward and in respect of expected benefits.'[7]**

Hence, it considers male as well as female children independent human beings to be brought up as ornaments of life and not mere chattels owned by the fathers - chattels which may be cashed or sold to acquire material benefit or compensation for loss of services. Therefore, Islamic discipline inculcates equitable treatment of children in a manner in which parents would expect their children to treat

---

[4] Genesis 29.20/21
[5] 1 Samuel 18.22/27
[6] Aid to Bible Understanding, Watch Tower Bible Society, p. 1114
[7] Al Quran 18.47

them.[8] And since parents would expect their daughters to treat them in a decent manner and with respect and equity - female offspring are commanded to be brought up as individual human beings enjoying the same rights and privileges as male children in strict conformity with the Islamic dictum:

'Be mindful of your duty to Allah and act equitably between your children[9]

The Islamic law of equity stipulates that parents respect the lives and honour of their female offspring. It demands that parents not give their sons preference over their daughters. The Prophet of Islam[sa] declared:

'He who has a daughter and does not bury her alive, nor humiliate her, nor give a son preference over her will be admitted to paradise."[10]

He also laid a particularly heavy stress upon the treatment of female offspring and repeatedly declared that parents who treat their daughters in a decent manner may expect to earn the pleasure of God and also be rewarded by Him. Traditions attributed to the Prophet Muhammad[sa] proclaim:

'A person who brings up two girls through their childhood will appear on the Day of Judgement, attached to me like two fingers of a hand."[11]

Islam is positively the only religion which glorifies the status of daughters to an extent that they are stated to act as a shield for their menfolk to save them from the chastisement

---

[8] Sahih Muslim 10.644
[9] Sahih Bukhari 47.13
[10] Masnad Ahmad
[11] Ibid.

of Hell. This is indicated in a Hadeeth which states that a person:

> **'who is tried with daughters and treats them well will find that they become his shield from the Fire.'[12]**

It also stresses upon teaching good manners to the female species[13] and insists upon the education of women - a right not restricted to blood relations but extended further to embrace the entire species irrespective of the recipient lineage, status or position in a society. The Prophet of Islam[sa] stressed upon the education of women at the lowest rung of the social ladder and declared that:

> **'If a man have a slave girl, and he give her good education and proper training and then set her free, such a one shall have double reward on the Day of Judgement.'[14]**

BRIDE PRICE OR DOWRY

In the Judaeo-Christian culture, a father alone stands to benefit from the bride price on account of the argument that he ought to be compensated for the loss of services of the daughter and for the trouble and expense he had to undergo in caring for and educating her.[15] Islam on the other hand takes this right to financial gain away from the parent and bestows it exclusively to the womenfolk in its society. The Quran counsels men to seek women in marriage only after committing a part of their wealth to them whether this be in

---

[12] Ibid., 73.18
[13] Ibid., 46.16
[14] Ibid., 62.13
[15] . Aid to Bible Understanding, Watch Tower Bible Society, p. 1114

cash or other gifts and even landed property. It also gives women an absolute right to receive dower from their husbands - for them to spend in whatever permissible manner desired or deemed fit by them. It states in relation to this:

'Seek them in marriage, by means of your properties, not committing fornication. For the benefit that you may receive from them, pay them their dower as fixed.'[16]

In Islamic law, the father is denied access to any portion of the dower paid to his daughter by her husband while the husband is explicitly forbidden to demand or spend any part of it. However, a woman has been given the right to remit any part of the dower received by her from her husband to him if she so desires:

'There will be no sin upon you in respect of anything that you mutually agree upon after fixing the dower.'[17]

Nonetheless, the Quran is extremely insistent that any such mutual agreement whereby a wife decides to remit any part of her dower to her husband should be based upon the pleasure of the wife:

'Give women their dowry willingly. But if they on their own pleasure, should remit a part thereof, then enjoy it as something pleasant and wholesome.'[18]

Men are also commanded not to seek to marry women with a dower less than what other women of their social standing may command in the society.[19] Those men who are unable to

---

[16] Al Quran 4.25
[17] Ibid
[18] Ibid 4.5
[19] Sahih Bukhari 44.7

marry free women on account of financial disability or poverty are advised to marry from amongst the female slaves or prisoners of war. But they may do so only after a reasonable dower has been agreed and also according to what is fair. The Quran insists on this and states:

> **'Whoso of you cannot afford to marry from amongst free believing women, let him marry out of those believing women who have passed into your hands as hand maids. Allah knows your faith best; you are spiritually akin to one another. You may marry them with the leave of their masters and pay them their dowers according to what is fair.'[20]**

Islamic law is extremely insistent that a dower must be paid to free women as well as female slaves and prisoners of war even if it be in the form of educating the bride[21] or manumitting her if she be a slave or a prisoner of war.[22] Refugee women who leave their husbands to find security amongst Muslims have not been granted a right to secure a dower only but if Muslim men wish to marry them, they are commanded to pay compensation to their infidel husbands - thus imposing an additional burden upon the financial resources of a man whose only intention in seeking such a bond in matrimony may be out of sympathy. Yet, the Quran lays down the law to state:

> **'O ye who believe, when believing women come to you as Refugees, satisfy yourselves as to their faith. Allah knows well their faith. Then if you find them true believers, send them not back to the disbelievers. These women are not lawful for**

---

[20] Al Quran 4.26
[21] Sahih Bukhari 62.51
[22] Ibid., 62.14

them, nor are they lawful for these women; but remit to their disbelieving husbands what they spent on them. Thereafter, it is no sin for you to marry them on payment of their dowers.'[23]

Islam admonishes Muslim men not to curtail this right of women[24] or seek to deny them their due by making convenient arrangements where a female member of the family is given as a bride unto another in exchange of a female member of the other to avoid payment of dower to the two brides.[25] A practice of this nature or any other kind of trick devised to deprive women of their dower has been thoroughly condemned in Islam. Guardians of women have been advised against it[26] and Islamic law insists that a marriage cannot be legalised without the payment of a dower to the bride - a dower which could be as little as an iron ring[27] or as much as a heap of gold[28] depending upon the financial circumstances of the parties involved.

RIGHT TO RETAIN DOWER

Before the advent of Islam, the Arabian people were notorious for devising schemes of extracting money from their wives whom they wished to divorce. They would bring false charges of adultery or gross immorality against their spouses and often compel them to obtain divorce at the cost of huge retribution. Islam rooted this evil out by demanding a high standard of honesty and integrity in dealing with women. Hence, husbands are commanded by Law not to unnecessarily slander their wives nor expect any part of the

---

[23] Al Quran 60.11
[24] Sahih Bukhari 62.17
[25] Ibid., 86.4
[26] Ibid., 86.8
[27] Ibid., 62.15
[28] Ibid., 62.50

dower already promised or given to them. The Quran also demands that if a married couple prove incompatible and the husband desires to marry another woman, then he ought not calumniate his wife nor entertain any evil design of repossessing the gifts already presented to her lest he commit a manifest sin. It lays down strict injunctions to ensure that a woman's right under such conditions is not violated and states:

'If you desire to take a wife in place of another and you have given one of them a treasure, take not back aught therefrom. Will you take it by calumny and manifest sin? How can you take it when you have consorted together and they have taken from you a strong covenant?'[29]

A husband who wishes to end his relationship with a wife and who for whatever reason seeks a divorce is required by Islamic law not to prolong the agony of the estranged spouse in a hope that he may be able to extract some wealth out of her. He is therefore admonished:

'O ye who believe, it is not lawful for you to inherit women against their will, nor should you detain them wrongfully that you may take part of that which you have given them.'[30]

Islam has established a woman's absolute right to retain her own wealth including the dower gifted to her by her husband even where she is accused of adultery and consequently divorced on suspicion of it. Islamic law maintains that if the husband's allegations against his wife are false, then he has no right to demand the dower and if these are true, than he has already received the benefit of matrimony from his

---

[29] Al Quran 4.21/22
[30] Ibid., 4.20

accused partner.[31] A person who mistakenly marries a woman from amongst the forbidden degree of consanguinity is required by Law to divorce her on receiving knowledge of it. But, Islamic law stipulates that he cannot demand the return of the dower paid to her at the time of marriage.[32] These injunctions of the Shariah not only safeguard the right of women to retain any material wealth which they acquire from their husbands during the course of their marriage but, also secure them against the fear of losing their privileges in the event that their marriage goes sour.

INDEPENDENT EARNING AND ACCUMULATED WEALTH

Islamic law gives a woman the right to benefit financially from the wealth of her husband while at the same time it also safeguards her right to independent earnings and accumulated wealth. It states that:

> **'Men shall have a share of that which they earn and women shall have a share of that which they earn.'[33]**

The Quran also gives women an absolute right to own and retain whatever property they acquire through their own efforts or else either receive as gift or inherit within their own right - totally independent of their husbands. Men are commanded not to covet anything these women rightfully receive as a right from their parents, relatives or husbands and they are also under legal obligation to ensure that whatever belongs to women by right is restored unto them:

---

[31] Sahih Bukhari 63.30
[32] Ibid., 63.51
[33] Al Quran 4.33

> 'Covet not that whereby Allah has made you
> excel over others. Men shall have a share of that
> which they earn, and women shall have a share
> of that which they earn. Ask Allah alone of His
> bounty. Surely Allah has perfect knowledge of
> all things. For everyone leaving an inheritance,
> Wfe have appointed heirs, parents and near
> relations and also husbands and wives with
> whom you have made firm covenants. So give all
> of them their appointed shares. Surely Allah
> watches over all things.'[34]

It cautions men not to have any ulterior designs on what has already been gifted to women even under circumstances where their marriages are under severe strain and the possibility of divorce is being contemplated:

> 'O ye who believe, it is not lawful for you to
> inherit women against their will, nor should you
> detain them wrongfully that you may take part
> of that which you have given them.'[35]

It admonished men to deal kindly with women and cautions them that if for any reason they dislike their wives, it may be possible that they dislike something in which God has placed much goodness. Nevertheless, if they are unable to reconcile themselves to their partners, then Islam counsels them to release their wives in a permissible manner with honour and not demand back anything which they have already given or gifted to them. It states:

> 'If you desire to take a wife in place of another
> and you have given one of them a treasure, take
> not back aught therefrom. Will you take it by

---

[34] 4.33/34
[35] Ibid., 4.20

91

calumny and manifest sin? How can you take it when you have consorted together and they have taken from you a strong covenant.'[36]

Therefore, women possess an absolute right to hold whatever wealth they have accumulated during the period of their marriage and men are warned that it is unlawful for them to demand anything back from their wives:

'It is not lawful for you to take away anything of that which you have given to your wives.'[37]

Women are also under no obligation to transfer any part of their personal wealth including their dower to their husbands. Nor can their husbands demand that they do this unless women choose to do so willingly and at their own pleasure:

'Give women their dowry willingly. But if they on their own pleasure, should remit a part thereof, then enjoy it as something pleasant and wholesome.'[38]

Islamic law also grants women a right to guard their personal wealth and be extremely protective about their independent earnings. They are permitted to spend their wealth in whatever lawful manner they desire and men are not entitled to even demand that their wives assist them with the financial expenditure of maintaining their own household against their consent.[39] If women willingly assist their husbands of straitened means with contribution towards the household expense, then their assistance is stated to merit a double reward for them.[40] As against this, a woman has been given a right over her husband's wealth and property to spend from

---

[36] Ibid., 4.21/22
[37] Ibid., 2.230
[38] 38. Ibid., 4.5
[39] Sahih Bukhari 24.43
[40] Ibid., 24.47

it according to the needs of the household in a just and a reasonable manner.[41]

This right granted to women in the early years of Islamic history was not known to the Judaeo-Christian civilization until late 19th century. In Britain for instance, except for the City of London, women did not have a free disposal of their own earnings and the husbands possessed an absolute right to demand, collect and spend the labour of their wives. Even where a husband deserted his wife or forced her to leave the matrimonial home, her employer was legally obliged to pay him the remuneration of her employment if he so demanded.[42] According to the English Common Law, all real property which a bride held at the time of her marriage became the possession of her husband who was entitled to the income from her land and any profit which might be made from operating the estate during the joint life of the spouses. The husband's right on the property of his wife was absolute and he could spend it as he saw fit.'[43]

In Germany, women did not earn this right until after the Civil Code of 1900. But even after this period, the relative freedom of German women did not actually release their property from the administration of and use by their husbands.[44] In the United States of America, the traceable formal beginning of women's liberation movement did not occur until the middle of the last century. Yet, it wasn't until the early twenties of this century that women won the first phase of their battle to earn civil rights for themselves. They did not acquire legal parity to earn an equal amount of money as men until the sixties of the present century and as in Britain, an American woman's property was owned by her husband.[45]

---

[41] Ibid., 64.4
[42] Encyclopedia Britannica
[43] Encyclopedia Americana
[44] Woman's Mission and its Aim
[45] Sabet, Mostapha. The Role and Status of Women

Islam, on the other hand, granted this right to woman without any restrictions or reservations some fourteen centuries earlier. As soon as a woman attains majority, Islamic:

> 'law invests in her all the rights which belong to her as a human being. Her earnings acquired through her own exertions can not be wasted by a prodigal husband, nor can she be ill treated with impunity by one who is brutal. She acts *sui juris,* in all matters relating to herself and her property is her individual right, without the intervention of her husband or father. She can sue her debtors in open courts, without the necessity of joining a next friend or under cover of her husband's name. She continues to exercise, after she is passed from her husband's home, all the rights which the law gives to men.'[46]

INHERITANCE

Women are known to have been deprived a right to inherit property from their kith and kin in nearly every pre-Islamic civilization and religion while Islam opens every avenue of inheritance to them - whether they be daughters or wives and even mothers or sisters. It's Law of Inheritance stipulates:

> 'For everyone leaving an inheritance, We have appointed heirs, parents and near relations and also husbands and wives with whom you have made firm covenants. So give all of them their appointed shares. Surely Allah watches over all things.'[47]

---

[46] Woman's Mission and its Aim
[47] Al Quran 4.34

94

It does not permit the distribution of more than one third of one's wealth in legacies[48] nor does it sanction the share of heirs to be increased or decreased through testamentary directions.[49] The Quran lays down strict injunctions to ensure that none is deprived of one's right to inheritance while it protects a woman's right to inherit from her kith and kin:

> **'For men, as well as for women, there is a share of that which their parents and near relatives leave; whether it be little or much - a share which has been determined by Allah.'[50]**

To ensure that neither survivor is deprived of the rightful share, the Quran gives specific instructions regarding the proportionate distribution of the estate to state:

> **'Allah commands you concerning your children. A male shall have as much as the portion of two females.'[51]**

This distribution of a larger share to the male issue has often been exploited to the detriment of Islam but the injunction that male offspring receive a larger proportion is not without its own wisdom. Islam imposes the principal responsibility for the welfare of a family on the shoulders of a man and therefore he is subjected to a much greater financial responsibility[52] while a woman is free from any such financial commitment even if she is a lady of means.[53] In addition to this a man is taxed with additional commitments which the financial resources of a woman are not burdened with, as for instance, payment of a dower to the spouse.[54] There is

---

48 Sahih Bukhari 51.2
49 Ibid., 51.6
50 Al Quran 4.8
51 Ibid., 4.12
52 Ibid., 4.35
53 Sahih Bukhari 24.43/47
54 Al Quran 4.25

however no legal stipulation which forbids the parent from distributing an equal share to the daughter from the one third share which one is permitted to distribute as legacies from one's wealth. Nevertheless, where there are no male issues to inherit the wealth of a deceased, daughters automatically acquire a much larger share without any unnecessary restrictions imposed upon them as placed by Biblical law upon daughters who inherit the property of their fathers in the absence of male heirs.[55] The Quran stipulates that:

> **'If there be only females, two or more, they shall have two thirds of what the deceased should leave and if there be only one, she shall have one half.'[56]**

In addition to her absolute right to inherit from the estate of her parents, a woman's right to inherit from her deceased husband's wealth, whether he is or is not survived by a male issue, is also protected by Islamic law:

> **'They shall have a fourth of that which you leave, if you have no child; but if you have a child then they shall have an eight of that which you leave.'[57]**

A mother and a sister also benefit financially from the estates of a son and a brother as do a father and a brother:

> **'His parents shall have each of them, a sixth of the inheritance, if he have a child, but if he have no child and his parents be his heirs, then his mother shall have a third; but if he has brothers and sisters, then his mother shall have a sixth.'[58]**

---

[55] Numbers, 36.8
[56] Al Quran 4.12
[57] Ibid., 4.13
[58] Ibid., 4.12

The right of sisters to inherit from the estates of their brothers is further extended by the Quran to enable them to inherit from the estates of their sisters also as well as their paternal half brothers and sisters:

> 'If a man dies leaving no child and he has a sister, she shall have half of what he leaves; and he shall inherit her if she has no child. But if there be two sisters, then they shall have two thirds of what he leaves. And if the heirs be both men and women, then the male shall have as much as the portion of two females.'[59]

Sisters who share a common mother with other brothers or sisters are also not denied a right to inherit from their maternal half brothers or sisters:

> 'If there be a man or a woman whose heritage is to bedivided and he or she has no parent nor child, and he or she has a brother and a sister, then each of them shall have a sixth. But if they be more than that, then they shall be equal sharers in one third.'[60]

Islam is extremely insistent that female offspring, as much as their male counterparts, should not be left in dire financial conditions. In situations where there is only one female heir, parents are not permitted to bequeath more than one third of their wealth to charity[61] although traditions suggest that this proportion of one's property bequeathed to charity is also rather excessive.[62]

---

[59] Ibid., 4.177
[60] Ibid., 4.13
[61] Sahih Bukhari 23.35
[62] Ibid., 80.6

The Islamic law of Inheritance also protects the rights of second generation female issues as much as it protects the rights of second generation male issues in situations where the parents die before the grandparents.[63] Where a person is survived by a daughter, a sister and a female grandchild, the Law gives the right of inheritance to all three female relatives of the deceased.[64]

In addition to all this protection granted to women to ensure that they are not deprived of their right to inheritance, Islam also gives women a unique right to sue for their rightful share if they feel ever that they have been short changed in matters of inheritance or otherwise by their menfolk.[65] Traditions indicate that Muslim women successfully sued their menfolk during the lifetime[66] of Prophet Muhammad[sa] and also in the subsequent history of Islam without any fear of reprisal.[67] This right which was hitherto unknown to the Arabian society was also not known to have been given to women by any pre-Islamic religion nor by any post Islamic secular civilization until the present century.

EDUCATION

The quest to acquire knowledge has been given great priority in Islam and the Quran commands Muslims to constantly supplicate:

> **'Lord, bestow upon me an increase of knowledge.'[68]**

---

[63] Ibid., 80.7
[64] Ibid., 80.8
[65] Ibid., 54.2
[66] Jami Tirmidhi
[67] Sahih Bukhari 54.2
[68] Al Quran 20.115

It also states that of the servants of Allah, it is those who possess knowledge that fear Him[69] and that Allah shall exalt those to whom this bounty has been bestowed.[70] The need to seek and acquire knowledge is therefore a duty imposed upon every man and woman, irrespective of one's social standing in a society or one's financial position[71] and a person who strives to educate him or herself is considered to be one absorbed in the cause of Allah.[72]

Islam also maintains that people who follows the path of knowledge will find their way to Paradise eased by the Lord.[73] It states that a believer is never content with the knowledge that has been acquired until he or she ends up in Paradise[74] and Traditions report that the Prophet of Islam[sa] declared:

> **'For one who adopts a path seeking knowledge, Allah eases the way to Paradise and the angels spread their wings for the seeker of knowledge, being pleased with one's occupation, and all that are in heaven and the earth, including the fish in water ask forgiveness for such a one. A learned person is superior to the worshipper as the moon is superior to all the planets.'[75]**

The quest to acquire knowledge is only one aspect of a believer's duty in Islam which also considers dispensing of knowledge the best of charity. It makes it incumbent upon every learned person to spread knowledge[76] not only to those that are present but also to those who may be absent.[77] Muslims who acquire knowledge and then teach others are

---

[69] Ibid., 35.29
[70] Ibid., 58.12
[71] Sunan Ibn Majah
[72] Jami Tirmidhi
[73] Sahih Muslim
[74] Jami Tirmidhi
[75] Sunan Abu Daud
[76] Sahih Bukhari 3.10
[77] Ibid., 3.38

considered superior human beings[78] and Prophet Muhammad[sa] declared:

> **'A learned one is as much above the worshipper as I am above the least of you. Allah, His angels and all those in heaven and the earth, even the ants in their heaps and the fish in water call down blessings upon those who instruct people in beneficent knowledge.'[79]**

Prophet Muhammad[sa] is also reported to have stated that there are only two kinds of persons to be envied in this world - one upon whom Allah bestows riches and gives power to spend in a righteous cause and the other upon whom He bestows wisdom to judge and teach others.[80] Therefore, Islam has laid an extremely heavy stress upon the need to seek, acquire and dispense knowledge while before the advent of Islam, nearly every known civilization considered it unnecessary to educate women in its society because their only brief in life was to serve the physical needs of their men and bear children. In the Hebrew cultures, the female species were not given a defined right to pursue education nor to dispense knowledge. The Judaic scriptures maintain absolute silence on this question but its ordinances in relation to the rights and obligations of women give sufficient evidence to indicate that they did not have a right to enter the field of education nor were they permitted to educate others. The Christian scriptures on the other hand explicitly restrict women from engaging themselves in this field:

> **'Let the women learn in silence with all subjection. But I suffer not a woman to teach,**

---

[78] Ibid., 3.21
[79] . Jami Tirmdhi
[80] Sahih Muslim

nor usurp authority over a man, but be in silence.'[81]

The New Testament places severe restrictions upon a woman's quest to acquire knowledge and her desire to broaden the horizons of her intellectual capacity. It denies her the right to publicly request clarification or elucidation of points not understood by her. If she fails to understand an issue, she is prevailed upon to continue holding peace until she reaches home where she may ask her husband to assist her:

'Let your women keep silence in the churches; for it is not permitted unto them to speak; but they are commanded to be under obedience, as also saith the law. And if they will learn anything, let them ask their husbands at home; for it is shame for women to speak in the church. What! came the word of God out from you? or came it unto you only?'[82]

These restriction are placed upon the female species to assert male authority and keep women in subjugation to their menfolk - a fact admitted by the exponents of the Christian faith who state that Saint Paul:

'laid down as a rule that women must not be allowed to speak in public congregation, or to assume the office of teachers or disputants; for this by no means consisted with the obedience to their husbands which the law of God inculcated. But if they met with anything in the public instruction which they could not understand or assent to, let them wait till they come home, and

---

[81] 1 Timothy 2.11/12
[82] 1 Corinthians 14.34/36

ask their husbands about it, who are supposed able and willing to inform them and who are the most proper persons for them to confer with.'[83]

This justification of Biblical injunctions which place unnecessary restrictions upon the female species in a Christian congregation insults the intellectual capacity and competence of women. It also assumes that all men are endowed with better intellectual capacity and are intellectually superior to women. Therefore, they are thought to be more competent and in a better position to understand public instructions being given in the Christian congregation. Hence, women who fail to understand any part of what they hear in the church are admonished to maintain silence in public and approach their men in the privacy of their homes who on account of their allegedly better intellectual capacity would be able to enlighten them further.

Islam does not restrict this right to acquire and dispense knowledge to the menfolk in its society only. The education of women has been given high priority and Muslims have been commanded to educate, not only their own female offspring, but also the other women in their charge including slaves girls. Traditions report that Prophet Muhammad[sa] stated:

'If a man have a slave girl, and he give her good education and proper training and then set her free, such a one shall have a double reward on the Day of Judgement.'[84]

The practical implementation of this advice is more than evident in the earliest history of Islam. It's Prophet[sa] set aside a particular day to educate Muslim women in the tenets of Islam and also Islamic thought and philosophy which

---

[83] Scott. Illustrated National Family Bible, p. 1109
[84] Sahih Bukhari 62.13 **Ibid**

embraces every aspect of knowledge from personal hygiene to the creation of the world.[85] His Companions[ra] also took particular care to convey the Holy Prophet's[sa] sermon to women.[86] This interest shown in educating women produced remarkable results and Muslims are to this day thoroughly indebted to their female spiritual ancestors for the knowledge that has been passed down to them through the efforts of these great female scholars and educationalists of the early Islamic history.

For instance, Ayesha bint Abu Bakr[ra] was and is held in high regard for her vast knowledge and understanding of the Quran and Islamic jurisprudence. She is regarded a scholar comparable to the second and fourth caliphs of Islam, Umar ibn Khattab[ra] and Ali ibn Abi Talib[ra] and also 'Abd Allah ibn Abbas[ra] and 'Abd Allah ibn Mas'ud[ra] who were, within their own, right four of the greatest Muslim scholars.

Ayesha's[ra] judgements on questions of Islamic jurisprudence are considered flawless and impeccable[84] unto this age and she was often consulted by Muslims whenever they encountered a difficulty in relation to any question of Islamic law or Sunnah which for Muslims is an ideal mode of conduct in life.[85] She is reported to have even corrected Muslim scholars of repute whenever they misinterpreted Quranic verses[86] and men of exceptionally high scholastic and intellectual ability are recorded to have declared that there was never an occasion that they consulted Ayesha bint Abu Bakr[ra] on a crucial question and she was not able to enlighten them.[87] Her analysis of Muhammad[sa] is considered of great value by Muslims scholars even unto this age. She was also well versed in poetry, history and even medicine[88] and she is believed to have taught more than two hundred Muslim

---

[85] Ibid., 92.9 **Sahih Bukhari 22.26**
[86] Ibid., 3.33 **Ibid 40.21**
[87] Masnad Ahmad vol. 6, pp. 306/307 **Jami Tirmidhi**
[88] Sahih Bukhari 71.8

students of whom some became great scholars of Islam within their own right.[89] In fact, it may not be an exaggeration to state that Ayesha bint Abu Bakr[ra] was one of the greatest scholars ever produced by Islam.

Hafsha bint Umar[ra] was also a great scholar within her own right. Prophet Muhammad[sa] personally took great interest in her education[90] and she became so well versed in Islamic knowledge that she could academically discuss and argue finer and delicate points of the Quran with men of such calibre as the Prophet of Islam[sa] himself.[91] She is also known to have dispensed knowledge to some of the greatest men in the history of Islam including scholars of such renown as 'Abd Allah ibn Umar[ra].

Umm Salama bint Abi Umayya[ra] was yet another Muslim lady whose opinion was often sought on questions of Islamic jurisprudence and the practice of Prophet Muhammad[sa] by male Muslim scholars who were within their own right Companions[ra] of the Prophet of Islam[sa] and who had not only learnt Islam first hand but also witnessed the practical conduct of the Prophet of Islam[sa] within his lifetime.[92] Her verdict on questions of Islamic jurisprudence carried more weight than the verdict of some of the greatest Muslim scholars known to the history of early Muslims[93] and her knowledge benefited such scholars of Islam as Abu Huraira[ra] and 'Abd Allah ibn Abbas[ra] - two of the greatest Muslim scholars and traditionalists.[94] She is acclaimed for her profound insight and perception and considered a great jurist of her time[95] as well as a remarkable educationalist whose list

---

[89] Masnad Ahmad vol. 6, p. 312
[90] Ibid, p. 281
[91] Ibid, p. 285
[92] Sahih Bukhari 22.26
[93] Masnad Ahmad vol. 6, p. 306
[94] Ibid, p. 312
[95] Ibid, p. 217

of student include such renowned personalities as 'Abd ar Rahman ibn Abu Bakr[ra] and 'Urwa ibn Zubair[ra].

Safiyya bint Huyyai[ra], a Jewish convert to Islam became a centre of education within her own lifetime and women from as far as Kufah approached her to question her on points of Islamic law and jurisprudence.[96] She acquired this extensive knowledge after her conversion to the faith of Islam. Sauda bint Zam'aa[ra] influenced such scholars of repute as 'Abd Allah ibn Abbas[ra] and 'Abd Allah ibn Zubair[ra] and also Ayesha bint Abu Bakr[ra] who remained ever grateful to her throughout her life.[97] Umm Maimuna bint Harith[ra] was also a scholar within her own right and often enlightened Muslim scholars of such high repute as 'Abd Allah ibn Abbas[ra] who respected her judgements on questions of Islamic jurisprudence.[98] Umm Habiba bint Abi Sufyan[ra] exercised a great influence upon such men of renown as Mu'awiyah ibn Abi Sufyan[ra], later the founder of the Umayyad dynasty and her judgements on questions of Islamic law and practice was universally respected by Muslim men.[99] Umm Sulaim bint Milhan[ra] was yet another Muslim lady who often approached Prophet Muhammad[sa] to enlighten herself on questions of Islamic law[100] and her views were often sought and respected by Muslim scholars. She is even stated to have solved differences of opinions between such scholars of repute as Hasan ibn Thabit[ra] and 'Abd Allah ibn Abbas[ra] - two of the greatest Muslim scholars and traditionalists known to the history of Islam.

Umm Waraqa bint 'Abd Allah[ra] memorised the Quran during the lifetime of Prophet Muhammad.[sa] She taught the Sacred Scriptures and led women in prayer while 'Asma bint Abu

---

[96] Ibid p. 377
[97] Tabaqat Ibn Sa'd, vol. 8, p. 37
[98] Masnad Ahmad vol. 6, p. 331
[99] Ibid, p. 326
[100] Sahih Bukhari 73.68

Bakr[ra] had a lasting influence upon her own sons as well as second generation Muslims.[101] 'Asma bint Umais[ra] was within her own right an extremely educated women, much sought for her knowledge of the interpretation of dreams. Umm Aiman bint Tha'lba[ra] exercised great influence over 'Anas ibn Malik[ra] who is acknowledged to be one of the greatest traditionalist and scholars known to Islam as did Umm Fadhl bint Harith[ra]. Umm 'Atiyya bint Harith[ra] dispensed knowledge to Muslims in Medina as well as Basra where she migrated. She even corrected second generation Muslims in matters relating to innovation in the faith of Islam and her verdicts on such sensitive matters as the seclusion of women was respected by Muslim men.[102] Umm Darda bint Abi Hudard[ra] is also considered an intelligent and educated woman of sound judgement by Muslim scholars of repute and Umm Hani bint Abi Talib[ra] is also stated to have been a scholar of Islamic jurisprudence within her own right.

Rabi' bint Ma'udh[ra] was a great scholar of Islamic jurisprudence and her opinion was sought by such scholars of repute as 'Abd Allah ibn Abbas[ra]. Fatima bint Qais[ra] was thoroughly well versed in Islamic jurisprudence and her personal influence extended well beyond the period of the early caliphate into the Umayyad dynasty. Khansa bint 'Umar[ra], a renowned poet of her age left behind a treasure in her field which was published not only in Arabic but was also translated in some European languages. Zainab bint Abi Salama[ra] is believed to be one of the greatest female scholars of Islamic jurisprudence known to her age. Shifa bint 'Abd Allah[ra] was reputed for her knowledge of herbal medicine and her perfection in the art of calligraphy and 'Asma bint Yazid[ra] is stated to have been endowed with extreme intellect.

---

[101] Sahih Bukhari
[102] Ibid, 15.20

These are but a few Muslim women who acquired a high standard of education in the early years of Islamic history and who dispensed education to the first and the new generation of Muslims - including some of the greatest male scholars known to the history of Islam. In fact, never in the history of mankind has a single nation ever produced such a large percentage of female intellectuals and as was produced by Islam in its early years. The impact of the intellectual influence these women exercised in their society was felt so acutely that during the period of Umar ibn Khattab[ra], female education was made compulsory and women were encouraged to attend lectures and sermons.

This right given to Muslim women in the early years of Islamic history some fourteen centuries ago was not granted to women in the allegedly more advanced Biblical orientated western world until the twentieth century. Nonetheless, even after women in the western hemisphere secured this right to acquire knowledge, they did not receive parity with men in the field of education until the later part of the century. In the United States for instance, sex discrimination in education was not banned by an act of the Congress until 1972.

FREEDOM OF SPEECH AND RIGHT TO EXPRESS OPINION

Biblical scriptures have been shown to restrict a woman's freedom of speech and its injunctions demand that women receive instructions in submission and obedience to their menfolk. They are commanded not to teach or usurp a man's authority[103] and if they fail to understand an issue they are instructed to observe silence until they reach home where they may ask their husbands to assist them because it is considered shameful for them to speak in public as, allegedly,

---

[103] 1 Timothy 2.11/12

the word of God did not descend upon them but was given unto them.[104]

Islam gives women a unique right to request elucidation of matters which they fail to understand properly[105] and thereafter continue demanding further explanation until the issue is properly understood by them.[106] They are free to seek clarification of the requirements of Islamic law and even raise such questions in relation to these as may embarrass their menfolk.[107] Women have been known to constantly exercise this right from very early in the history of Islam[108] while their menfolk are known to have felt shy to seek advice on issues of similar nature.[109] They have sought clarification of Islamic law in relation to menstruation[110] and feminine bleeding not related to menses[111] as well as nocturnal emissions[112] or otherwise and Traditions indicate that they did so much to the embarrassment of their menfolk but without fear of censure or reprehension.[113]

Islamic convention grants women an absolute right not to only pursue knowledge but also enlighten others. Women are free to teach in an Islamic society and they may dispense knowledge to either species. Hence, a sizable number of Muslim women were able to acquire an exceptionally high standard of education in the early history of Islam and thereafter dispense knowledge to some of the greatest male scholars known to its history. Men of such renown as 'Abd Allah ibn Zubair[ra], Anas ibn Malik[ra], 'Abd Allah ibn Umar[ra] and Jabir ibn 'Abd Allah[ra] owe a great debt to Muslim women as

---

[104] 1 Corinthians 14.34/36
[105] Sahih Bukhari 3.36
[106] Ibid 3.37
[107] Ibid 6.16
[108] Ibid 3.51
[109] Ibid 3.52
[110] Ibid 4.67
[111] Ibid 6.10
[112] Ibid 5.23
[113] Ibid 73.68

do 'Abd Allah ibn Abbas[ra], a scholar of high repute and Abu Huraira[ra], one of the greatest Muslim traditionalists.[114]

Muslim women have also been given the right to advise men on the question of permissibility in Islamic law[115] as well as non-permissibility of certain actions.[116] Their influence extended far beyond the borders of Arabia[117] - within the lifetime of Prophet Muhammad's[sa] companions[118] and also beyond the periods of the righteous caliphs.[119] They are known to have settled points of difference between some of the greatest male scholars known to the history of Islam who are said to have felt obliged to withdraw their verdicts on question of Islamic jurisprudence in favour of the verdict issued by Muslim women. These male scholars are also known to have admitted that women who corrected their opinions possessed a far superior knowledge of Islam.[120] Muslim men are also known to have often approached women to be enlightened on questions of Islamic law and convention[121] and it has been stated in relation to one such female scholar often approached by them:

'It never happened that the companions of Muhammad[sa] consulted Ayesha[ra] on a difficult matter and she was not able to enlighten us.'[122]

Traditions also indicate that in the field of knowledge, Muslim women suppressed their shyness to enlighten their menfolk on certain extremely embarrassing issues.[123] They also had the courage to not only interfere in personal matters of some

---

[114] Masnad Ahmad vol. 6, p. 312
[115] Sahih Bukhari 6.5
[116] Masnad Ahmad vol 6. p. 332
[117] Sahih Bukhari 6.25
[118] Masnad Ahmad vol. 6, p. 307/307
[119] 119. Ibid p. 217
[120] Ibid pp. 306/307
[121] Sahih Bukhari 22.26
[122] Jami Tirmidhi
[123] Sahih Bukhari 6.7

of the most powerful families who ignored certain Islamic laws or conventions but they had the confidence to challenge some of the mightiest Muslim rulers when the law of Islam was seen by them to have been ignored or broken.[124]

Islam also bestows upon its women a right to express their personal opinion without fear of their menfolk - a right often exercised by Muslim women. Ayesha bint Abu Bakr[ra] for instance had the courage to refuse expressing her gratitude to Prophet Muhammad[sa] after she was vindicated by God Almighty of a false rumour spread against her by the hypocrites in Medina. She argued that she was deeply indebted to God for having affirmed her innocence and had no reason to express her gratitude to her husband.[125] Such a response would have been considered outrageous under ordinary circumstances but Ayesha[ra] comments at such a crucial stage in her life and Prophet Muhammad's[sa] admission of these as valid are evidence of how bold Muslim women had become under the influence of Islam and how much freedom of speech men in a Muslim society permitted their women after the advent of Islam.

In another incidence when her husband[sa] expressed his disapproval in a certain family matter, Ayesha[ra] responded by quoting the Quran: 'This is through the bounty of Allah. He bestows it upon whosoever He pleases' and the Prophet[sa] immediately withdrew his objection.[126] This is yet another indication of the freedom of speech which Muslim women enjoyed under Islam - freedom which not only permitted them to speak freely but also assert their right when their husbands disapproved of their actions.

On yet another occasion when she was found to be suffering from a headache, Prophet Muhammad[sa] humoured her by

---

[124] Ibid 63.41
[125] Ibid 59.33
[126] Sahih Bukhari

stating to her that she ought to be cheerful because if she died, he shall prepare her coffin with his own hands and bury her himself after saying funeral prayers and supplicating for her salvation. She retorted to this in a similar tone of humour and stated: 'And when you come back, you will bring here another bride in my place.'[127] Although stated in humour, she may have never had the courage to respond in a manner in which she did had Muslim women not been accustomed to speaking their mind on account of the right given to them by Islam.

Traditions indicate that she not only showed the courage to freely speak her mind in the presence of her husband[sa] but she also had the boldness to rebuke Muslim men at random whenever she felt that the rights of Muslim women were being threatened.[128] She had the courage to even challenge some of the mightiest Muslim rulers if she felt that the rights of women were being abused and the conduct of the rulers was against the spirit of Islam.[129]

Ayesha bint Abu Bakr[ra] was not the only woman who possessed the courage to disagree with Prophet Muhammad[sa] on certain matters relating to personal conduct of minor significance[130] as well issues of intellectual importance.[131] She was also not the only Muslim woman known to have had the courage to respond to her husband without fear of being penalised for being so outspoken.[132] Umar ibn Khattab[ra], known for his stern disposition as much as for his sense of justice and fair play often found his wife responding to him in the same manner in which he behaved towards her.[133]

---

[127] Ibn Hisham, Sirat al Nabi
[128] Sahih Bukhari 9.13
[129] Ibid 63.41
[130] Ibid 60.303
[131] Masnad Ahmad vol. 6, p. 285
[132] Sahih Bukhari 60.316
[133] Ibid 43.26

Although feared by the women of Medina[134] - yet women did not fear him enough not to express their opinion in his presence or exercise their right of free speech within the confines of decency and decorum. They protected their personal freedom[135] and their right to privacy in family affairs[136] from male scrutiny even to the extent that they responded to men in an abrupt manner.[137] In later years, Muslim men commented upon how they had authority over their womenfolk[138] in pre-Islamic days of ignorance and how they treated them with indifference until God bestowed unique rights upon them.[139]

Women have also been given a right to complain about the conduct of their husbands in their personal lives[140]- a right which they have exercised so fearlessly that their menfolk have often taken exception and even expressed anger at the bluntness of their wives.[141] Women in a thoroughly Islamic environment enjoyed this right to free speech to an extent that men began to not only complain that their wives had become insolent but they also sought permission to chastise them.[142] Nevertheless, they continued to exercise their unique rights during the periods of the succeeding caliphs and even challenged the mightiest of Muslim rulers when they felt that their rights were under threat. For instance, a woman who took exception to Umar ibn Khattab's[ra] attempts to restrict the amount of dower paid to Muslim brides stood up to challenge his authority is attempting to restrict what the Quran had made lawful. She recalled his attention to the Quranic verse 4.21 and stated: 'O son of Khattab! How dare

---

[134] Sahih Muslim
[135] Sahih Bukhari 60.241
[136] Ibid 60.316
[137] Ibid
[138] Ibid 43.26
[139] Ibid 60.316
[140] Ibid 48.3
[141] Ibid 72.6
[142] Ibn Majah

you deprive us when God says in the Quran that even a heap of gold may be settled on the wife as a dower.' Umar[ra] publicly appreciated the courage of this woman and complimented her by saying:

'The women of Medina have better understanding of Islam than Umar.'[143]

RIGHT TO EXERCISE DISCRETION

Islam also bestows upon women a unique right to exercise discretion in personal matters as well as issues of national importance and significance. Women released from slavery are given an option to either retain their husbands imposed upon them during their days of bondage or else leave them if they prefer not to spend the rest of their lives with men forced unto them by their masters during the period of their bondage.[144] Women also reserve the right to either seek advice of their parents or else refuse to consult them in matters of significant matrimonial importance even when such consultation is being suggested by their husbands.[145] They have been granted discretion to use funds from the wealth of their husbands if they feel that their partners are not being fair in the expenditure of the household[146] and they are also entitled to show compassion towards their pagan relatives and provide them with shelter under exceptional circumstances. They may guarantee these infidels safe haven much to the annoyance of their menfolk but Islam honours their word and endorses their guarantee given to infidels.[147]

---

[143] Sahih Bukhari
[144] Ibid 63.14
[145] Ibid 60.237
[146] Ibid 64.4
[147] Ibid 8.4

CONFIDANTS AND COUNSELLORS

Islamic convention not only grants women a right to free speech but it also elate their status as confidants and counsellors in whom men confide their secrets and whose advise is placed in high regard by their menfolk even when not sought. The Prophet of Islam[sa] established this convention himself when he confided in his wife Khadija bint Khuweilid[ra] at the time when the doors of Divine revelation were first opened unto him. She advised him to consult her cousin Waraqa ibn Naufal[ra] and seek explanation of his experience - an advice to which Prophet Muhammad[sa] eagerly responded.[148] Khadija[ra] remained a trustworthy confidant and sincere counsellor to the Prophet of Islam[sa] for nearly twenty five years of her life and her advice was always a source of great comfort to him.[149]

Prophet Muhammad[sa] continued to confide in his wives throughout his life even though on some occasions they did not justify the confidence which he placed in them.[150] Traditions also indicate that he accepted counsel of his wives even when it was not sought as for instance when his directions to his Companions[ra] to slaughter their sacrificial animals and shave off their heads was met with scanty attention at Hudaibiyya. His wife Umm Salama[ra] who had noticed the signs of grief on his countenance comforted him and advised him not to say anything to his Companions[ra] since they were overborne with sorrow at the unequal terms of the treaty which Muslims had just signed with the infidels of Mecca. She ventured to suggest that he should slaughter his own sacrificial animals and shave his head so that following his example his companions may do likewise.[151]

---

[148] Sahih Bukhari 1.1
[149] Asad al Ghaba, vol. 1
[150] Al Quran 66.4
[151] Sahih Bukhari

One can well imagine the emotional state of Prophet Muhammad[sa] at that point in time when his orders were not immediately responded to. He had left Medina with a cavalcade of some fifteen hundred Muslims hoping to perform his religious rites at the Ka'aba. After a long and arduous journey, he was made to camp at Hudaibiyya by the Meccans who swore that they would not allow him and his party to proceed any further nor would they let Muslims enter the holy precincts at Mecca. He had to sign a treaty with the infidels the terms of which were considered humiliating by his Companions[ra] and for the first time in his life they had not only argued with him on the wisdom of accepting such terms but also paid scanty attention to his orders.[152] Any ordinary person would have immediately rebuked his spouse to hold her peace and not interfere in matters of such national importance but the Prophet of Islam[sa] was an embodiment of all the virtues which Islam proposed to inculcate in its society. He approved of the suggestion made by his wife and emerging from the tent, proceeded to put her advice into effect. As the Muslims saw him, they immediately followed his example and an extremely tense situation was satisfactorily resolved on the advice of a woman gifted with incredible intellect and perception by God Almighty.

Women continued to be confidants and counsellors to Muslim men even after the demise of Prophet Muhammad[sa] in matters of religious[153] as well as social[154] and national importance.[155] Ayesha bint Abu Bakr[ra] was approached by such men of influence as Talha ibn Ubaidullah[ra] and Zubair ibn Awaam[ra] on the question of Ali ibn Abi Talib's[ra] refusal to take immediate action against the assassins of Uthman ibn Affan[ra]. Hafsha bint Umar[ra] advised 'Abd Allah ibn Umar[ra], son

---

[152] Ibid
[153] Ibid 22.26
[154] Ibid 6.25
[155] Masnad Ahmad

of the second caliph Umar ibn Khattab[ra] on the course of action he should adopt after the battle of Siffin.[156] 'Asma bint Abu Bakr's[ra] valuable advice was frequently sought by 'Abd Allah ibn Zubair[ra] when the Muslim nation was engaged in civil strife after the assassination of Hasan ibn Ali ibn Abi Talib[ra]. Traditions indicate the these women exercised an exceptional influence over their menfolk during these periods and their advice on questions of national importance was highly regarded by men.

ADMISSIBILITY OF EVIDENCE

Biblical law appears to make absolutely no provision whatsoever to permit the admissibility of female evidence in any sphere of life. However, Islam is the first religion which gives women the right to bear witness in commercial as well as social spheres of life. The Quran states that whenever Muslims engage in a commercial transaction they ought to commit the agreement in writing and also:

> **'Procure two witnesses from among your men; and if two men be not available, then one man and two women, of such as you like as witnesses, so that if either of the two women should be in danger of forgetting, the other may refresh her memory.'[157]**

The fact that in this injunction the testimony of two women has been held equal to one man has often been exploited to the detriment of Islam to suggest that it discriminates against women. Nevertheless, in the first instance, such an objection being made by someone whose own religion does not make any provisions for the admissibility of a woman's evidence is

---

156
157 Al Quran 2.283

a height of mockery. Secondly, it should be observed that the Quran clearly gives its reasons as to why two women are required to bear testimony in such cases against an accepted standard of one man:

> **'so that if either of the two women should be in danger of forgetting, the other may refresh her memory.'**

In normal circumstances, a woman is safeguarded against the prospect of having to appear as a witness in any kind of a judicial proceeding particularly if she be a hostile witness to either of the two parties. Yet, since this rule is relaxed in an emergency, it may result in certain unforeseeable difficulties which may arise on account of the social structure which Islam has created for its society. A male witness who attests a document has a greater chance of his memory being regularly refreshed about the transaction when he socially meets the other concerned parties since the custom of such transactions being recalled at social meetings was in vogue in Arabia.

However, under an Islamic system, women do not socialise with men to the extent that men do amongst themselves and the prospect of their memory being regularly refreshed in relation to an agreement which they attested is somewhat slim. To overcome this impediment, the Quran stipulated that where only one male witness is available - two female witnesses may be called upon to attest a document so that if one was to forget then the other may be able to refresh her memory. In the words of one of the greatest jurists the world has seen in our present century:

> **'This provision is concerned only with the preservation of the evidence, and does not concern the weight to be attached to the testimony of a male or female witness. An**

illustration may help to clear up any doubt on the matter. Assume that a transaction recorded in a document attested by one male and two female witnesses becomes a subject of dispute which comes up for judicial determination. It is then discovered that one of the two female witnesses has since died. The male witness and the surviving female witness are examined in court and the judge finds that their respective accounts on the terms of the transaction are not entirely in harmony; but he feels very strongly that taking every relevant factor into consideration, the testimony of the female witness is more reliable than that of the male witness. In such a case, it would be his plain duty to rely on the testimony of the female witness in preference to that of the male witness. There could be no question of discrimination in favour or against a woman."[158]

The admissibility of the evidence of one woman has also been accepted by Islam even when the testimony is in relation to an offence committed against the woman herself and she is a female slave.[159] Islam regards the evidence of women including female slaves in such high esteem that their testimony is admissible in determining the validity of a matrimonial bond [160] and marriages already solemnised and consummated are subject to be annulled on the basis of their evidence[161] if such evidence cannot be conclusively refuted[162]

---

[158] Khan, Muhammad Zafrullah. Women in Islam, p. 18
[159] Sahih Bukhari 83.7
[160] Ibid 48.14
[161] Ibid 48.13
[162] Ibid 48.4

and even if the husband involved in a case of this nature considers the female offering evidence as a liar.[163]

Evidence of a single female in cases of assault is also admissible[164] and a penalty of death may be pronounced against the offender in the event that the victim dies as a result of the injury sustained in an assault.[165] Women have a right to give evidence in relation to the character of other women also, whether the witness be a free woman of noble stock[166] or else a female slaves.[167]

RIGHT TO REDRESS

Women in the pre-Islamic civilizations did not have a right to redress if any injustice was done to them by their menfolk. In a Biblical society, women could be deprived of an opportunity to acquire the wealth of their deceased husbands[168]; abducted from their homes and subsequently raped and widowed[169]; defiled by their own half-brothers[170]; violated by a depraved mob throughout the night on account of the cowardice of their male host and husbands and finally butchered to pieces[171] and also falsely accused of improper conduct and adultery by a jealous husband and consequently subjected to public humiliation and physical pain.[172] Yet Biblical law does not make any provision for these women to be either compensated for the offence against their person

---

[163] Ibid 62.24
[164] Ibid 83.7
[165] Ibid 83.5
[166] Ibid 60.213
[167] Ibid 48.15
[168] Genesis 38.11
[169] 2 Samuel 11.4/7
[170] 2 Samuel 13.11/20
[171] Numbers 5.11/31
[172] Judges 19.24/29

nor does it give them the satisfaction of seeing their assailant punished for the actual offence against them.

In matrimonial matters also, Biblical husbands appear to have all the rights they need to treat their wives in whatsoever manner they consider fit or expedient and while the law permits a husband to merely hand a Bill of Divorce to his wife and turn her out of the house[173], a wife is not given any such right to seek divorce.

Islam on the other hand give equal rights to women in every sphere of life. They are protected from physical abuse and attack in the society and their assailant can be punished with the penalty of death.[174] They are also given an opportunity to vindicate themselves against false charges of impropriety brought against them and not only does their oath of innocence carry more weight than the charge of guilt against them[175] but their accuser can be sentenced to public lashing and turned into a social leper.[176] Furthermore, women are granted absolute freedom to sue their menfolk if ever they feel deprived of their right.[177]

Hence, Islam has bestowed such secular rights upon the female species as not known to any other religion. It is through Islam that women came to own and possess personal wealth and property by right and not default. It is through the interest which Islam took in the education of the female species that women came to enlighten themselves intellectually and consequently they became great scholars and educationalist. It is Islam that gave them a right to free speech and an opportunity to express their opinion or exercise their discretion without fear of recrimination. It is Islam which gave women an opportunity to become confidants of and

---

[173] Deuteronomy 21.1
[174] Sahih Bukhari 83.7
[175] Al Quran 24.7/11
[176] Sahih Bukhari 48.22
[177] Ibid 54.2

counsellors to men as much as it gave respectability to their evidence. It is positively, the only religion which gave women a right to redress any injustice meted upon them. No religion or civilization has done so much for so many in such a short span of time as Islam did in some two decades of the noble Prophet Muhammad's[sa] ministry.

All praise belongs to Allah!

CHAPTER FIVE

THE CONCEPT OF MOTHERHOOD

A woman could assume multiple roles within the span of her lifetime - from a daughter to a sister and a wife to a mother. But amongst all these varied roles, the role of the mother is the first recognised by any human being since it is she who carries the burden of an unborn child and nurtures it within her own body for a period of nine months before it sees the light of the day. She then suckles the infant through childhood and weans the child into adolescence but throughout this period and ever after, the mother remains every concerned of the welfare and happiness of her offspring. A mother has therefore traditionally commanded a considerable amount of reverence and respect in almost all known civilization of the world.

In the Judaeo-Christian cultures, the status of a mother has been recognised since ancient times but while Biblical laws forbid a man from uncovering the nakedness his father's wife[1] and also condemn a person who violates his father's bed to death[2] yet one observes that the Judaeo-Christian scriptures have drawn an extremely conspicuous line between one's own mother and the mothers of one's half or step brothers and sisters[3] not only during the pre-Covenant period but also after the Law had been expounded unto Moses at Sinai.[4] Consequently, as a result of this distinction, the sanctity of a father's other wives beside one's own natural mother has often been ignored in the history of the best and the noblest Biblical families.

Reuben - the eldest son of Jacob and his wife primary Leah[5] defiled and profaned his own father's bed when he committed incestuous immorality with Bilah[6] whom his father Jacob had taken unto himself as a wife.[7] Yet, while the entire nation heard of it, none dared censure his conduct and Reuben continued to enjoy the privilege of being Jacob's son.

Ahithophel, an adviser to David and grandfather of his secondary wife Bathsheba[8] is stated to have been a sagacious man whose counsel was esteemed as if it were a direct word of the Lord Yahweh.[9] Yet, to possibly avenge David's forceful abduction of his granddaughter, Ahithophel advised David's son Absalom to go in unto the concubines of his father so that all Israel shall hear and therefore the hands of all that are with Absalom be strong. Biblical evidences suggests that Absalom disregarded the honour of his father and his wives

---

[1] . *Leviticus 18*.8
[2] Ibid 20.11
[3] Genesis 43.29
[4] Judges 8.19
[5] Genesis 29.32
[6] Ibid 35.22
[7] . Ibid 30.4
[8] 2 Samuel 11.3 & 23.34
[9] Ibid 16.23

and even the strict penalty prescribed by Judaic law for such an offence but instead took Ahithophel's advice and:

> **'went in unto his father's concubines in the sight of all Israel."[10]**

MARY - MOTHER OF CHRIST

Biblical mothers continued to be looked upon with scorn and contempt in the time of Jesus Christ who addressed Mary as woman[11] throughout his life but never as mother even unto his death.[12] Christian apologists who justify this sad and extremely disrespectful mode of address adopted by their saviour admit that after Jesus reached maturity, he did not permit his mother to exercise paternal authority over him and that whenever she attempted to exercise her right, he held her in check[13] as for instance at a wedding at Cana when he somewhat abruptly rebuked his mother and stated:

> **'Woman, what have I to do with thee?"[14]**

Jesus's abrupt response to his mother and the manner in which he addressed her is admitted by his own followers to:

> **'sound harsh and almost repellent in their roughness and brevity.'[15]**

On another occasion when Jesus was informed that his mother awaited to speak to him as he addressed the crowd - instead of granting Mary her request he preferred his disciples

---

[10] Ibid 16.21/22
[11] John 2.4
[12] Ibid 19.26
[13] . Boettner, Loraine. Roman Catholicism, p. 199   14. John 2.4
[14]
[15] Farrar, Frederic W. The Life of Christ, p. 119

over her and hence humiliated his mother in fully view of a large multitude as evident from the following passage of the New Testament:

'While he yet talked to the people, behold, his mother and his brethren stood without, desiring to speak to him. Then one said unto him, Behold, thy mother and thy brethren stand without, desiring to speak with thee. But he answered and said unto him that told him, Who is my mother? and who are my brethren? And he stretched forth his hand towards his disciples, and said, Behold my mother and my brethren! For whosoever shall do the will of my Father which is in heaven, the same is my brother and sister and mother.'[16]

Jesus's response to his mother's anxiety to speak to him on this occasion and his refusal to grant Mary her request has once again been admitted by his own followers to have been a serious public rebuke. They state that when Mary sent word to him by messenger, making known her desire that he would come to her:

'Instead of granting Mary's request, he replied in such a way that it was in effect a public rebuke. Undoubtedly she felt it keenly.'[17]

It is universally admitted by almost all Christian scholars that Mary did not exercise influence or authority over her son. They cite this public rebuke of a mother by her son Jesus as example to state that if Mary had exercised any influence and authority over her son Jesus then:

---

[16] Matthew 12.46/50
[17] Boettner, Loraine. Roman Catholicism. p. 22

'He would not have answered her as he did but he would have honoured her request promptly.'[18]

In fact, Biblical evidences suggest that Jesus held motherhood itself in extreme contempt and this is clearly indicated by his response to a woman who stated to him:

'blessed is the womb that bore thee, and the breast that nursed thee.'

One would have expected a son to feel pride in his mother being blessed in such a manner by a stranger yet Jesus responded to these blessings with a retort:

'Rather blessed are they who hear the word of God and keep it."[19]

MOTHERHOOD IN ISLAM

Islam on the other hand has elated the status of a mother to enviable heights of honour and glory - whether she be a believer or an infidel. The tradition of denying the wives of the fathers the respect worthy of them had been the curse of the pre-Islamic Arabian custom. The Arabs considered only those women to be their mothers through whose loins they had taken birth and any other women who happened to be married to their fathers were denied the status of motherhood. Therefore, on a father's death, the heirs had a legal right to inherit their step mothers as well as the concubines in their harems as a part of their legacy. These women could then be prevailed upon to either become wives to their step sons or else concubines in the harems of the sons of their deceased husbands. They could also be gifted

---

[18] Ibid p. 201
[19] Luke 11.27/28

to other kinsmen of the deceased or else disposed of at the pleasure of the heirs.[20]

Islam put a stop to this abominable practice by clearly putting all women unto whom a father had gone beyond the permissible limits of physical liaison for a son and the Quran stated in relation to this:

'Marry not those women whom your fathers had married. What has passed has passed. It was a foul and hateful practice and an evil way. Forbidden to you are your mothers.'[21]

Islamic law gave a totally new meaning to the status of motherhood in so much that it not only placed step mothers and their off springs beyond the permissible limits of women lawful unto to the sons but it also placed foster mothers and their daughters amongst the list of women forbidden to foster children. The Quran admonished Muslims that forbidden it is for them to marry their:

'foster mothers that have given you suck, and your foster sisters.'[22]

Islamic thought is extremely insistent that Muslims honour not only those women whom their fathers had married since they are related to them as mothers being the spouses of their fathers but also their foster mothers and it states that:

'Foster relations make all those things unlawful which are unlawful through corresponding blood relations.'[23]

---

[20] 20. Sahih Bukhari 85.6
[21] Al Quran 4.23/24
[22] Ibid 4.24
[23] Sahih Bukhari 62.28

Muslims are therefore warned that all those things which are considered illegal in blood relationship are also considered illegal in foster relationship.[24] They are forbidden to marry persons suckled by a common wet nurse[25] and also the issues of such persons[26] since these women are considered as close in relationship as blood relations[27] and their children as one's own brothers or sisters[28] and even children.[29]

Islam also demands that a marriage contract between a couple suckled by a common foster parent be considered null and void[30] and where one is married in ignorance, a divorce is considered in order[31] when the knowledge of the facts become known to the parties concerned.[32] The Prophet of Islam[sa] advised couples who approached him for judgement in relation to such marriages by stating:

'How can you keep her as your wife when it has been said that you were foster brother and sister. Divorce her.'[33]

RESPECT DUE TO A MOTHER

Islam enjoins benevolence towards one's parents[34] and the Quran commands Muslims to deal gently with them and also invoke the mercy of God upon them because they nurtured them in infancy.[35] To show gratitude to one's parents has been declared to be the second most important duty imposed

---

[24] Ibid 60.242
[25] Ibid 62.24
[26] Ibid 62.21
[27] Ibid 62.27
[28] Ibid 62.24
[29] Ibid 62.34
[30] Ibid 48.14
[31] Ibid 48.13
[32] Ibid 48.4
[33] Ibid 62.24
[34] Al Quran 29.9
[35] Ibid 17.24/25

upon mankind - second only to one's duty to show gratitude to God and the Quran states in relation to this:

> 'We have enjoined upon man concerning his parents. Be grateful to Me and thy parents. His mother bears him in travail after travail, and his weaning takes two years.'[36]

While both parents are mentioned in this passage, a specific mention of the mother suggests that she has secured a special place in the Almighty Lord's affections - a fact substantiated by Hadeeth which state:

> 'Allah created the universe and when He had finished, the womb stood up and said: Is this the place of that which seeks thy protection against being cut off? Allah said: Yes. Would you be content that I should hold with him who holds with thee and should cut off with him who cuts off with thee? It said: I am content. Allah said: Then this is thy station. He who holds with thee shall I hold with him, and he who cuts thee off shall I cut off.'[37]

Islam exhorts Muslims to show goodness to their parents and fulfil their duty to them since it is considered second to Salat and better than Jihad.[38] To lack a sense of duty towards parents is considered one of the greatest sins - as grave as associating partners with God or infanticide.[39] Yet, Traditions indicate that a mother has been given a much superior right to duty by her children as indicated by the Hadeeth which declares:

---

[36] Ibid 31.15
[37] Sahih Muslim
[38] Sahih Bukhari 73.1
[39] Ibid 73.6

> **'Allah has forbidden you to be undutiful towards
> your mothers, to withhold from them what you
> should give them and demand from them what
> you do not deserve.'[40]**

In Islamic discipline, a mother is stated to be three times better entitled to kind treatment and good companionship than the father[41] and Muslim children are commanded to continue showing respect to them even after they are themselves married and become parents to their own children and therefore relatively independent.[42] Islam also demands that a duty to the mother should not only be fulfilled within her lifetime but also after her death[43] and if a mother should die without fulfilling any of her vows then Islam imposes a duty upon her children to fulfil her commitments.[44] These injunctions of the Quran and demands of the Hadeeth indicate that a woman and a mother has been given a far superior right to the affection and respect of her children - far above the right that has been given to a man and the father. This is indicated yet once again by a specific mention of the mother in another Quranic passage wherein it is stated:

> **'We have enjoined upon a man to act
> benevolently towards his parents. His mother
> bears him in pain and brings him forth in pain;
> and the bearing of him and his weaning extends
> over thirty months.'[45]**

In fact, Islam not only demands respect and benevolence towards one's own mother only but also requires that Muslims treat mothers of other people with respect also. It lays down

---

[40] Ibid 73.6
[41] Ibid 73.2
[42] Al Quran 46.16
[43] Sahih Bukhari 86.3
[44] Ibid 78.30
[45] Al Quran 46.16

strict injunctions against insulting mothers in general and considers any disrespect shown towards them a trait of pre-Islamic ignorance.[46]

HEAVEN LIES UNDER THE FEET OF A MOTHER

It has been shown that according to Biblical scriptures, it is perfectly normal and acceptable for one to show disrespect to one's own mother unless she conforms to the beliefs of her son and even when a son is disturbed by his mother while he is engaged in a religious duty. This is evident from Jesus's response to the woman who blessed the womb that bore him and the breast that nursed him[47] and also his public rebuke and denial of Mary when she sought to speak to him while he was engaged in preaching.[48] This insult meted upon his mother and also rejection of Mary by her own son Jesus is justified by Christian scholars on the grounds that:

> 'His disciples that had left all to follow him, and embraced his doctrine, were dearer to him than any that were akin to him according to the flesh. They had preferred Christ before their relations, they left their fathers, and now to make them amends, and to shew that there was no love lost, he preferred them before his relations; did not they receive, in point of honour, a hundredfold?'[49]

Islam on the other hand demands that a station of mother be honoured whether she is a believer or not. Muslim children of

---

[46] Sahih Bukhari 73.44
[47] Luke 11.27/28
[48] Matthew 12.46/50
[49] Henry. Illustrated National Bible, p. 922/23

heathen mothers who find themselves averse to entertaining them or accepting gifts from them on account of their disbelief are required by Islam to be kind, respectful and benevolent towards them despite their disbelief[50] and to ensure that they are neither apprehensive of entertaining their infidel mothers nor negligent in their duty towards them, the Quran states:

'Allah does not forbid you to be kind and act equitably towards those who have not fought you because of your religion, and who have not driven you forth from your homes. Surely, Allah loves those who are equitable.'[51]

Traditions report that Prophet Muhammad[sa] not only commanded his followers to show respect towards their mothers irrespective of whether they had embraced Islam or not but also maintain good relations with them[52] and be good to them[53] - a right which Muslims never denied their parents but instead continued to be respectful towards them despite the painful attitude of their pagan parents.[54] Abu Huraira's[ra] mother for instance is stated to have been often disrespectful towards the Messenger of God[sa] before she embraced Islam and although he was extremely grieved at her attitude yet in years to come he stated:

'By Allah in Whose hand my soul is, but for Jihad, Hajj and my duty to serve my mother, I would have loved to die a slave.'[55]

Islam expects a mother to be held in reverence since she bears her children in great agony and suffers incredible

---

[50] Sahih Bukhari 73.7
[51] Al Quran 60.9
[52] Sahih Bukhari 47.29
[53] Ibid 73.8
[54] Sahih Muslim
[55] Sahih Bukhari 46.16

physical pain and emotional anguish on account of them. This is why, unlike the Biblical Christ, Jesus who is stated to have been disrespectful to his mother, the Quranic Messiah, Isa[as] is declared to have been an obedient and a humble son of his mother as stated in the Quran:

'Jesus said: I am a servant of Allah, He has given me the Book, and has appointed me a Prophet; He has made me blessed wheresoever I may be, and has enjoined upon me Prayer and alms-giving so long as I live. He has made me dutiful towards my mother, and has not made me haughty and graceless.'[56]

While duty to one's parents comes second only to one's duty to God, the beauty of Islamic thought is that duty to one's parents is in fact considered duty to God and therefore Muslims are exhorted to give preference to them as against engagement in Jihad.[57] They are also discouraged from giving priority to anything else as against fulfilling the rights of their mothers since Islam maintains that:

'Paradise lies under the feet of a mother.'[58]

Islam therefore places every sincere Muslim's ultimate desire, the blessed reward of the righteous under the feet of a woman and Prophet Muhammad[sa] declared:

'The womb is suspended from the Throne of Allah and proclaims: Allah will hold him who holds by me, and, Allah will cut asunder from him who cuts asunder from me.'[59]

---

[56] Al Quran 19.31/33
[57] Sahih Bukhari 73.3
[58] Sahih Muslim
[59] Ibid

CHAPTER SIX

RIGHTS OF MARRIED WOMEN

Marriage, according to the Judaeo-Christian and Islamic cultures is regarded a sacred institution and none of these three sister faiths differ in their attitude towards the sacredness of the matrimonial contract. As in Judaism and Christianity, marriage in Islam has been described as a covenant between a husband and a wife[1] - subject to certain rights and obligations. But unlike Judaism where a husband is considered the owner of the woman and therefore the wife is required to remain in subjection to him she being his property[2] or Christianity where a wife is commanded to remain in subjugation to her husband even if he be an infidel[3] because she is stated to have been created for him and not he for her[4]

---

[1] Al Quran 4.22
[2] 2. Aid to Bible Understanding. Watch Tower Bible Society, p. 1115
[3] 1 Peter 3.1
[4] 1 Corinthian 11.8/9

- female spouses in Islam are considered partners to their husbands. The noble Quran states in relation to this:

> **'Of His Signs it is that He created mates for you from your own kind that you may find peace of mind through them, and He has put love and tenderness between you. In that surely are Signs for a people to reflect.'[5]**

Women in Islam are therefore equal partners in a marriage - created for the benefit of men as much as men are created for the benefit of women. Hence they enjoy equitable rights protected by such specific injunctions of the Quran as declare:

> **'Wives have rights corresponding to those which husbands have, in an equitable manner.'[6]**

While it is not denied that in Islamic thought, men have been appointed guardians over women[7] and have therefore been given a certain degree of advantage over them[8] yet this minimal advantage is subject to heavy responsibilities as indicated by the Traditions of the noble Prophet of Islam, Muhammad[sa] who admonished Muslims:

> **'Everyone of you is a guardian and is responsible for his charge. The ruler who has an authority over people is a guardian unto them and is responsible for them; a man is a guardian of his family and is responsible for them; a woman is guardian of her husband's house and children and is responsible for them and a slave is a guardian of the master's property and is**

---

[5] Al Quran 30.22
[6] Ibid 2.229
[7] Ibid 4.35
[8] Ibid 2.229

responsible for it. So all of you are guardians and therefore responsible for your charge.'[9]

Moreover, this minimal degree of advantage given to menfolk in an Islamic society does not in any manner whatsoever diminish the rights of women - rights which have been amply bestowed upon them by Islamic law and convention. They not only continue to hold an equitable position in the administration of the household and also the general conduct and welfare of the family but Islam acknowledges their lordship over their home and children[10] and also appoints them sole and rightful custodians of their households.[11] Therefore, women in Islam enjoy a certain degree of superiority over men in the administration of their household.

SANCTITY OF RIGHTS IN A MATRIMONIAL CONTRACT

Islam maintains that amongst the contracts which a man has to fulfil in his life, the marriage contract has the greatest right to be fulfilled.[12] It admonishes men that their wives have rights concerning them as much as they have rights concerning their wives[13] and it commands them to honour these in a similar manner in which they honour the rights of their own body and their own soul.[14] Islam also cautions men not to entertain rancour against their wives and should they dislike one quality in them, they should find another which is pleasing to them.'[15]

---

[9] Sahih Bukhari 46.17
[10] Ibid 62.91
[11] Ibid 62.82
[12] Ibid 50.6
[13] Jami Tirmidhi
[14] Sahih Bukhari 62.90
[15] . Sahih Muslim 8.576

Husbands are directed not to strive to acquire a higher standard of piety at the cost of the rights of their wives[16]and even though Islam places the remembrance of the Almighty God extremely high on the list of virtues which Muslims should constantly aspire to inculcate in themselves and the Prophet of Islam[sa] stated: 'By Him in Whose hands is my life, if you were to continue as you are, occupied in the remembrance of Allah, angels would shake hands with you in your beds and your streets' yet he declared that men should not ignore the rights of their wives.[17] Tradition also state that on one occasion, three people approached the wives of Prophet Muhammad[sa] and enquired about his practice in the matter of worship upon which one declared that he would spend the whole night in voluntary prayer while the second resolved to observe voluntary fast every day without interruption and the third vowed to keep away from women and never marry. When the Prophet of Islam[sa] received information of the resolve of these three men, he admonished them:

'I fear God more than you do and am more mindful of my duty to Him than you are. But, I observe the fast and also abstain from fasting, and I perform voluntary prayer at night and also sleep, and I consort with my wives. He who turns away from my practice is not one of me.'[18]

In yet another instance, a companion of Prophet Muhammad[sa] indulged in excessive spiritual exercises to observe the fast during the day and remain engaged in voluntary prayer during the night to the point that his wife began to feel neglected. She complained about this to one of her husband's friends who advised the husband that while it was true that he owed a duty to his Lord, yet he owed a duty

---

[16] Sahih Muslim
[17] Ibid
[18] Sahih Bukhari 62.1

to his wife also and therefore it was essential that he fulfil his obligations to both. He stated:

'Your Lord has a right over you, your soul has a right over you and your wife has a right over you. So you should render to everyone their due."[19]

The matter was eventually referred to the Prophet of Islam[sa] who pronounced judgement in favour of the wife and also advised his companion not to ignore her rights in favour of spiritual exercises[20] since Islam does not permit a husband's religious zeal to encroach upon the rights of his wife.[21] On the contrary, it requires husbands to show moderation in their duty to God[22] and fulfil their duty towards their wives[23] since they have as much right on them as their own souls and bodies have on them.[24]

TREATMENT OF WIVES

Islam demands that Muslim men ought not to consider their wives as either household servants or mere governess for children. The Quran admonishes them that women are:

'apparels for you as you are apparels for them.'[25]

The deep and penetrating wisdom of this passage has to be understood in its proper perspective for one to appreciate the high regard in which Islam has put wives as partners to their

---

[19] Ibid 31.52
[20] Ibid 73.86
[21] Ibid 73.84
[22] Sahih Muslim
[23] Sahih Bukhari 31.56
[24] Ibid 21.19
[25] Al Quran 2.188

husbands. The Quran has stated elsewhere that God Almighty has bestowed raiment unto mankind to cover its nakedness and also as a means of adornment.[26] It has also been stated that God has provided mankind with garments to protect it from the vicissitude of climate and also man made attempts to inflict harm upon each other.[27] When the above passage is studied in the context of these verses of the noble Quran, then it proposes to state that husbands and wives have been created for each other as objects of mutual protection, embellishment and comfort and they act as a cover for each other just as apparels cover a person's nakedness; as an embellishment for each other just as clothes adorn beauty and add lustre to a person's personality and also as a protection for each other as garments protect mankind from the vicissitude of climate and man-made attempts to inflict harm upon each other. Therefore Islam requires men to treat their wives with such respect and regard as is due to them and as behove the status of a Muslim and hence they are commanded to:

'consort with them in kindness.'[28]

Islam also maintains that women have been created by God Almighty with an extremely tender disposition[29] and it compares them to a crystal glass[30] which ought to be treated with extreme caution and gentleness.[31] It has also been stated in relation to women that:

---

[26] Ibid 7.27
[27] Ibid 16.82
[28] Ibid 4.20
[29] Sahih Bukhari 73.116
[30] Ibid 73.95
[31] Ibid 73.111

'A woman is like a rib, if you try to straighten it, you will break it. But if you let it be, it will be of benefit to you despite its bend.'[32]

Since Islam is also aware of the shortcomings of human nature, it admonishes Muslims not to be harsh in their treatment of their wives[33] but if they are displeased with one disagreeable quality in them, they ought to find pleasure in another which is more agreeable and it assures men that they are certain to find agreeable qualities in women.[34] The Quran itself draws attention of husbands to the risk of disliking their wives and states:

'if you dislike them, it may be that you dislike a thing wherein Allah has placed much good.'[35]

The treatment of wives has therefore been given high priority in Islam. Muslims have been admonished to show kindness towards women[36] and to deal with them in a polite manner.[37] Islam maintains that the most perfect of believers in the matter of faith is he whose behaviour is best and the best amongst them is he who behaves best towards his wife[38] and it also declares that the more civil and kind a Muslim husband is towards his wife, the more perfect he is in his faith.[39] It cautions men that women are their surety to eternal reward:

'Would you know that a woman deserves a greater reward than a man for verily, the Almighty Allah exalts the position of a man in

---

[32] Sunan Abu Daud
[33] Sahih Bukhari 55.1
[34] Sahih Muslim
[35] Al Quran 4.20
[36] Sahih Bukhari 62.83
[37] Ibid 62.80
[38] Miskat al Masabih
[39] Jami Tirmidhi

heaven because his wife was well pleased with him and prayed for him.'[40]

Yet, despite such demands of kind treatment of women, Islam has often been accused of permitting brutal treatment to wives.

LIGHT CHASTISEMENT A LAST RESORT

It is not to be denied that Islam permits light chastisement of wives and the Quran states in relation to this:

'Admonish those of them on whose part you apprehend disobedience and leave them alone in their beds and chastise them. then if they obey you, seek no pretext against them. Surely, Allah is High, Great.'[41]

This Quranic injunction has often been capitalised upon by high handed Muslims who find pleasure in being brutal to their wives as much as it has been exploited by antagonists to the detriment of Islam. Nonetheless, in the first instance one has to study the permissibility of this injunction in the light of the circumstances which necessitated the same.

It has already been shown that women in the pre-Islamic era suffered severe subjugation to their menfolk and spent their lives totally deprived of even their basic and fundamental human rights. But Islam turned the tables for them to bestow upon then such rights in every sphere of life that this sudden emancipation of their species was not easily contained by women and consequently their husbands began to complain that their women had become too arrogant.[42] Hence, under

---

[40] Jami Tirmidhi
[41] Al Quran 4.35
[42] Sahih Bukhari 62.94

these exceptional circumstances, Islam permitted husbands to discipline their wives but when one refers to the text of the passage which permitted them to resort to such action, one finds that in the first instance they are commanded to admonish their wives failing which their bed is to be separated and as a last resort they are to be lightly chastised. But on both these accounts the punishment cannot be allowed to go to the extremes since in the first instance Islam does not permit a husband to abstain from relationship with his wife for an indefinite period within the bonds of matrimony[43] since the maximum period of abstinence permitted in a marriage cannot exceed four months.[44] On the second score Islam demands that only such chastisement be taken recourse to as a last resort as is extremely light[45] and the Prophet of Islam[sa] stated quite clearly:

'You have a right in the matter of your wives that they do not allow anyone whom you do not like to come to your house; if they do this, chastise them in such a manner that it should not leave any impression.'[46]

This Tradition should sufficiently indicate that permission to chastise a wife as a last resort has been given only when her conduct is beyond ordinary defiance of the authority of the husband who has been entrusted the guardianship of the family and the responsibility to oversee its moral welfare. Otherwise Islam permits women to disobey their husbands if they are ordered to do anything sinful[47] and the Quran gives them permission to seek arbitration if they fear cruelty on the

---

[43] Al Quran 4.130
[44] Ibid 2.227
[45] Sahih Bukhari 62.94
[46] Jami Tirmidhi
[47] Sahih Bukhari 62.95

part of their spouses[48] and even demand separation and divorce if an amicable settlement cannot be reached.[49]

In normal circumstances however, Islam admonishes men not to chastise their women unnecessarily.[50] The Quran states quite clearly that men have been appointed guardians over women[51] and therefore they are responsible for the welfare of their womenfolk[52] and should take care of them.[53] Islam also imposes a duty upon men to provide for the needs of women as they provide for their own need[54] and it also demands that if some of their women:

'are afflicted with contrariness, retain them with forbearance and silence.'[55]

The Prophet of Islam[sa] was extremely insistent that the rights of women not be denied to them by their men. In his farewell address to Muslims a short while before his demise, he exhorted Muslims to treat women kindly and his parting words were:

'O ye people! you have some rights over your wives and your wives have some rights over you. They are a trust of Allah, placed in your hands so treat them with kindness.'[56]

It is also stated that he admonished Muslims so often in relations to the rights of women that his companions radically changed their attitude towards their wives 'lest far more stringent rules and commands be revealed and their social

---

[48] Al Quran 4.129
[49] Ibid 4.131
[50] Jami Tirmidhi
[51] Al Quran 4.35
[52] Sahih Bukhari 51.9
[53] Ibid 62.81
[54] Sahih Bukhari
[55] Sahih Muslim
[56] Ibid

status be enhanced still further.'[57] Traditions also indicate that after permission to inflict light chastisement upon wives was granted, women in Medina approached the Prophet of Islam[sa] to complain of ill treatment of their husbands at which he showed thorough annoyance with Muslims and even stated:

'You will not find these men the best amongst you.'[58]

Prophet Muhammad[sa] took an extremely grim view of wives being physically chastised by their husband and he is reported to have stated that:

'anyone to whom Allah has given authority over others and does not look after them in an honest manner will not smell the fragrance of Paradise.'[59]

He was quite insistent that Muslims husbands follow his advice in matters relating to the kind treatment of their wives and he declared that it was sinful for a man not to safeguard the rights of women. He stated:

'Allah! I declare sinful any failure to safeguard the right of two weak one – the orphans and women.'[60]

Islam is also so thoroughly considerate of the rights of wives that it forbids men from engaging in Jihad if their wives have resolved to perform Hajj. It advises husbands to accompany their wives to fulfil their spiritual duties rather than participate in Jihad even if Muslim forces suffer extreme shortage of fighting men.[61] It also forbids newlywed husbands to engage in Jihad particularly when their marriages have not been

---

[57] Sahih Bukhari 62.81
[58] Sunan Abu Daud
[59] Sahih Bukhari
[60] Sunan al Nasai
[61] Sahih Bukhari 52.181

consummated[62] and ordinances enacted by the succeeding caliphs required that wives of Muslim soldiers should not be separated from their husbands for a period of more than four months.

RIGHT TO REDRESS

It has already been shown that the Quran describes husbands and wives as garments for each other[63] and commands Muslims to deal with their wives graciously.[64] While it is not denied that it gives men a right to discipline their spouses yet recourse to light chastisement can only be taken as a last resort[65] and Traditions suggest that this right ought not to be used indiscriminately but resorted to only when women are guilty of improper conduct[66]

Nonetheless, women have been adequately protected against the excessive exercise of this authority by their menfolk and the Quran guarantees them a right to redress. In situations where women apprehend ill treatment or indifference on the part of their husbands, Islam gives them an absolute authority to seek redress against them[67] and while husbands are initially admonished to seek suitable reconciliation with their wives and be benevolent towards them[68] yet should such reconciliation through mutual consultation prove difficult Islam imposes an obligation upon the society to seek means of reconciling the differences between the couple. The Quran states in relation to this:

---

[62] Ibid 62.59
[63] Al Quran 2.188
[64] Ibid 4.20
[65] Ibid 4.35
[66] Jami Tirmidhi
[67] Sahih Bukhari
[68] Al Quran 4.129

> 'If you apprehend a breach between them, then
> appoint an arbiter from among his people and
> from among her people. If they desire
> reconciliation, Allah will bring accord between
> them. Surely, Allah is All Knowing, All Aware.'[69]

Muslim women have not only been secured against the threat of physical abuse by their husbands[70] but they have also been granted protection against emotional blackmail by their menfolk. Before the advent of Islam, it was a common practice amongst Arabs to resort to character assassination of women if they desired to get rid of them.[71] Islam ensured that this evil is rooted out in its society and the honour and piety of women is secured against verbal abuse. Therefore, the Quran accorded special protection to women against their character being assailed by men and stated:

> 'Those who calumniate chaste, unwary,
> believing women are cursed in this world and
> the hereafter, and for them is a grievous
> chastisement, on the day when their tongues
> and their hands and their feet shall bear witness
> against them as to what they used to do.'[72]

Islam strictly forbids the character assassination of women and represents such a practice to be one of the seven essential sins to be avoided by Muslims at any cost.[73]

---

[69] Ibid 4.36
[70] Sahih Bukhari 62.94
[71] Sahih Bukhari
[72] Al Quran 24.24/25
[73] Sahih Bukhari 82.31

CONSENT OF WOMEN

It is rather ironic that the predominantly Christian media in the West has often drawn a gory picture of the manner in which marriages in Islam are conducted on account of the Islamic tradition that parents or guardians assume responsibility of advising and selecting the prospective brides and bridegrooms for their wards. In a Judaeo-Christian society, it is customary for the fathers and guardians to not only seek a match for their children or wards[74] but also accept[75] or reject the overtures made by prospective candidates[76] and even stipulate conditions under which they would be agreeable to permit the marriage of their children.[77] While there is absolutely no indication whatsoever in Biblical literature to suggest that the consent of the girl whose marriage is being proposed is ever sought as a rule - there appears to be enough evidence to indicate that fathers made this arbitrary decision on their own without ever consulting their children.[78] There are also ordinances in Biblical law which give fathers a right to deny consent of marriage to their daughters even when their wards are confronted with the most unfortunate and pressing circumstances - such circumstances as may hamper the future prospects of their daughters being sought in marriage by other men.[79]

Islamic law requires guardians of women to arrange marriages of their wards including widows in the society as well as slaves retained by Muslims and the Quran states in relation to this:

---

[74] Genesis 24.3/7
[75] Ibid 29.18/19
[76] Ibid 34.8/14
[77] Ibid 34. 15/17
[78] 1 Samuel 18.17/19
[79] Exodus 22.16

'Arrange marriages of widows from among you, and of the righteous from among those under your control, male and female. If they be poor. Allah will grant them means out of His bounty.'[80]

Yet, this obligation is not a licence to disregard the wishes of women directly affected by the decision of the guardians. The sacred institution of matrimony has been designed to form a permanent bond of relationship between a man and a woman and as such requires extreme caution. Islam proposes to block all avenues as may cause a hindrance in sustaining a happy and harmonious relationship between the couple - till death did them part. Therefore, it has established an uncompromising criterion:

'O ye who believe, it is not lawful for you to inherit women against their will.'[81]

The consent of a woman is therefore essential in any proposed marriage or else a person who marries a woman against her will would be deemed to have gone against the aforementioned injunction of the Quran and therefore his marriage would be considered unlawful in Islam and be subject to annulment by authorities if ever contested by the woman in question.[82] This right of a woman to consent to matrimony with a particular individual has also been upheld in the Traditions of Prophet Muhammad[sa] which insists that:

'A widow shall not be married until she is consulted and a virgin shall not be married until her consent has been obtained.'[83]

---

[80] Al Quran 24.33/34
[81] Ibid 4.20
[82] Sahih Bukhari 85.4
[83] Ibid 62.42

A woman's absolute right to be consulted before any decision is made in relation to her and also her right to consent to a proposed match has not only been restricted to free women in an Islamic society but it has been extended to embrace female slaves and hence Islamic discipline demands that:

'a lady slave should not be given in marriage until she has been consulted and a virgin should not be given in marriage until her permission has been granted.'[84]

Islam gives a woman the right to refuse a proposal of marriage under which circumstances men are required to respect her wishes.[85] A marriage solemnised with a coerced consent of a woman is considered null and void[86] and a matrimonial contracts solemnised without the free consent of a ward may be subject to annulment.[87] The practical implementation of these rules was observed in the lifetime of Prophet Muhammad[sa] when a woman complained that her father had forced her to marry her cousin in order to raise his status in the society. She was given permission to dissolve the marriage and choose whoever she wished to marry at which she replied:

'O Messenger of Allah. I accept my father's decision but my only purpose was to let people know that I have a free choice in this matter.'[88]

This right granted to Muslim women in the early years of Islamic history continued to be upheld after the demise of the Prophet of Islam[sa] and women who felt apprehensive that their parents or guardians might force them into matrimony

---

[84] Ibid 86.
[85] 85. Ibid 63.39
[86] Ibid 62.43
[87] Ibid 85.4
[88] Sunan Abu Daud

without their consent and against their wishes had their fears alleviated by Muslim elders.[89] A woman influenced into giving consent retains the right to rethink her decision even after her marriage and if she finds that she is unable to reconcile to the bonds of matrimony due to reasons beyond her control then Islam permits her to exercise her right to annulment even if she cannot find a fault with her husband but is merely unable to reconcile to him on account of incompatibility or varying temperaments.[90] A husband is then not only required to respect the sentiments of his wife under such circumstances but he is advised to give her an honourable divorce if one is being sought by the wife.[91]

A freed slave also reserves the right not to remain with a husband imposed upon her by her master during the pre-Islamic era after her release from the bondage of slavery[92] and while men are permitted to intercede on behalf of their distraught husbands, women have an absolute right to make their own decision in relation to their future course of action. They may permit themselves to be influenced or refuse to accept their former husbands.[93]

Islam also gives women a right to solicit suitable suitors for themselves within permissible limits of decency.[94] They have a right to offer their own hand in marriage[95] and even present themselves for marriage to righteous men without fear of censure by the society.[96] Men are also admonished not to deny women their desire if they decide to get married[97] and the Quran states quite clearly:

---

[89] Sahih Bukhari 86.11
[90] Ibid 63.12
[91] Ibid
[92] Ibid 63.15
[93] Ibid 63.16
[94] Ibid 59.
[95] Ibid 62.33
[96] Ibid 72.49
[97] Ibid 62.37

'prevent them not from marrying their husbands if they agree between themselves in a decent manner.'[98]

It also demands that guardians of orphans and other weak women not impede them from marrying men of their own choice nor force them into matrimony under coercion.[99] This Quranic verse is stated to have been revealed to desist guardians from preventing their wards from marrying men of their own choice, a custom stated to have been in vogue in Arabia.[100] Therefore the common opinion that Islam denies women a right to make their own choice or disregards their expectations by forcing them into marrying total strangers is based either on misinformation or else sheer bias against Islam since Muslims have been discouraged from embarking upon this crucial event of their lives without proper investigation and personal satisfaction. Hence an expectation of compatibility is a pryerequisite to an Islamic marriage and this cannot be achieved without the satisfaction that the concerned couple considers itself compatible. Therefore, people intending to marry are advised to meet each other and be satisfied before finally arriving at this important decision in their lives.[101] Traditions indicate that Prophet Muhammad[sa] himself advised his followers not to engage into matrimony blindly but see their intended partner first[102] and determine as to what attracts them towards each other.[103] He was in fact quite insistent that one ought not engage one's self in this sacred bond without first having looked at the other person[104] since he was of the opinion that meeting each other

---

[98] Al Quran 2.233
[99] Ibid 4.128
[100] Sahih Bukhari 62.37
[101] Jami Tirmidhi
[102] Sahih Muslim
[103] Sunan Abu Daud
[104] Sahih Muslim

was likely to bring about greater love and concord between them.[105] He is also stated to have declared:

'You must look at the woman because if love is to spring between you, the two should see each other.'[106]

According to the Quran, God has created a man and a woman from a single soul[107] so that they may find comfort[108] and peace of mind in each.[109] But this comfort and peace cannot be realised unless the couple are compatible to each other or at least believe to be so. Therefore, Islam does not ignore the personal sentiments of human beings and hence it stresses upon the importance of marrying such persons only as may seem agreeable to one.[110] It also considers a marriage conducted under coercion invalid[111] and hence for any relationship to qualify as valid and permissible in Islam, the consent of the couple has to be essentially sought and they ought not be coerced into matrimony against their will.

Islamic thought also maintains that one who marries perfects half of one's faith[112] but such perfection cannot be expected unless the couple can relate to each other with love and affection and where a bond of matrimony is forced upon the parties concerned, the prospects of them being able to deal with each other in a decent and loving manner or fulfil their duty unto one another in a manner required by Islam may not be feasible. It is therefore essential that extreme caution be exercised in matrimonial matters and the sentiments of the couple involved be given full consideration for the marriage to be successful or else it would defeat the very

---

[105] Miskat al Masabih
[106] Jami Tirmidhi
[107] Al Quran 4.2
[108] Ibid 7.190
[109] Ibid 30.22
[110] Al Quran 4.
[111] Sahih Bukhari 85.
[112] . Miskat al Masabih

purpose for which God Almighty created a man and a woman, that is, to find comfort and peace of mind in each other.

Happily, Islam takes due stock of every aspect of human sentiments and personal likes and dislikes of individuals. Therefore, it protects the rights of Muslims before and after marriage and it considers this essential because Islam gives a marriage relationship as much importance as it gives to blood relationship. Hence, the Quran states:

'He it is Who has created man from water and has made for him kindred by descent and by marriage.'[113]

---

[113] Al Quran 25.55

CHAPTER SEVEN

THE INSTITUTION OF POLYGAMY

Polygamy, the practice of being married to more than one wife at the same time has been a long established custom and a recognised institution since ancient times. It has been widely practised by the elite and the sundry, believers and non-believers throughout the ages and it has not only been in vogue since the earliest recorded time but it has also been found positively permissible and justifiable in every society before the advent of Islam.

Lamech, a descendent of Adam through his fugitive son Cain is stated to have been the first polygamist of Biblical records. He had two wives at the same time[1] and not much later, the righteous sons of God, Adam's descendants through his son Seth also began to practice polygamy.[2] Abraham, the faithful friend of the Lord Yahweh was himself a polygamous man

---

1 Genesis 4.19
2 Ibid 6.2

since he married Sarah[3] as well as Hajar[4] and Keturah.[5] Biblical records indicate that he may have had some concubines also besides the three wives mentioned in Genesis although the number of these is not stipulated.[6]

Jacob alias Israel, the grandson of Abraham - the great progenitor of the Hebrew race and the consecrated son of Isaac was a thoroughly polygamous man. Although apologetically defended for having been tricked into polygamy by his father in law[7], Jacob was polygamous by choice and not deceit since within hours of his marriage to Leban's elder daughter Leah, he demanded his newly wedded wife's younger sister Rachel also whom he proceeded to marry a week later. He is then stated to have married Bilah and Zilpah, the maids of his primary wife Leah and his secondary wife Rachel.[8] Biblical evidences suggest that he abstained from multiplying his wives beyond the four only because of a compromise forced upon him by his father-in-law after Jacob had fled the land of Leban but was pursued by his father-in-law.[9]

PERMISSIBLE IN BIBLICAL SCRIPTURES

Moses, the great Biblical prophet who expounded the law for the posterity of Israel after its deliverance from bondage in Egypt did not impose any restrictions on this long established practice of his ancestors nor did he express any prohibitions as regards the continuance of this age old custom. On the contrary, he issued instructions on how to regulate polygamy

---

[3] Ibid 11.29
[4] Ibid 16.3
[5] Ibid 25.1
[6] Ibid 25.6
[7] Aid to Bible Understanding, Watch Tower Bible Society, p. 1116
[8] Genesis 29.23/30.9
[9] Ibid 31.50

in a proper manner. For instance, the law which he expounded stated:

> **'Thou shalt not uncover the nakedness of a woman and her daughter, neither shall thou take her son's daughter, or her daughter's daughter to uncover her nakedness; for they are her kinswomen ~ it is wickedness. Neither shall thou take a wife to her sister, to vex her, to uncover her nakedness; besides the other in her lifetime."[10]**

Some Biblical commentators assume that this verse contains an express prohibition of polygamy, arguing that the word sister merely signifies the wife which a person had already married. There is however no passage in the Scriptures which favours this view. On the contrary, Biblical law expounded by Moses rather than restrict polygamy makes allowances for it and also lays condition for its' regulation as for instance it states that if a man:

> **'take him another wife; her food and raiment and her duty of marriage, shall he not diminish."[11]**

Besides demanding that a polygamous man not ignore the rights of his earlier wives, the Law covenant also protects the rights of children born in a polygamous household.[12] These obligations imposed upon a polygamous husband to protect the rights of his multiple wives and also children born of his secondary spouses establishes the permissibility of polygamy within the Biblical law or else a person's secondary wives and their children would be considered outside the institution of legal marriage and therefore defined as concubines and

---

[10] Leviticus 18.17/18
[11] Exodus 21.10
[12] Deuteronomy 21.15/16

illegitimate issues in which event Israel's entire posterity through his secondary wives Rachel, Bilah and Zilpah would be considered outside the congregation of the righteous since the Biblical law clearly states that a bastard shall not enter the congregation of the Lord even unto his tenth generation.[13]

In fact, the very conduct of the succeeding Israelite prophets and national leaders bears ample evidence that the Hebrew race continued to honour this ancient institution and Israel's posterity continued to follow in the footsteps of its ancestors. Gideon, one of the greatest Israelite judges is stated to have begotten seventy one sons of his many wives and one concubine[14] and Elkanah of Ramathaim-zophim, the father of the great Israelite prophet Samuel was a polygamous man.[15] David, the great Israelite king also married a chain of wives. He is stated to have been married to Saul's daughter Michal[16] when he proposed to and married Abigail, the widow of Nabal the Carmelite[17] as well as Ahinoam the Jazreelitess.[18] Biblical evidences suggest that he also married Maacah daughter of Talmai, king of Geshur as well as Haggith, Abital and Eglah.[19] After he settled in Jerusalem, David continued to marry other women and also took unto himself several concubines.[20] He also married Bathsheba after she conceived an illegitimate seed of him[21] and conservative estimate maintain that he maintained harem of ninety nine wives and concubines.

His son Solomon, himself a son of David's secondary wife Bathsheba is believed to have been given the divine charge to keep the commandments of Yahweh by walking in His ways and by keeping His statutes and His commandments.

[13] Ibid 23.2
[14] Judges 8.30/31
[15] 1 Samuel 1.1/2
[16] Ibid 18.27
[17] Ibid 25.42
[18] Ibid 25.43
[19] 2 Samuel 3.3/5
[20] Ibid 5.13
[21] Ibid 11.27

His strict obedience to the Lord is stated to have endeared him so much to Yahweh that he was named Jedidiah by the Lord, meaning, the beloved of Yahweh. Yet, he set an all-time record with seven hundred wives and three hundred concubines of all colours, creeds and nationalities - Egyptians, Moabites, Ammonites, Edomites, Sidonian and Hittite and Ethopians.[22]

David's grandson and Solomon's son Rehoboam fathered twenty eight sons and sixty daughters of his eighteen wives and sixty concubines[23] while Jesus's own foster father Joseph was also a polygamous man since his mother Mary was Joseph's secondary wife.[24]

POLYGAMY NOT RESTRICTED BY CHRIST

Although Christian apologists often argue that since God's original standard for mankind was for a husband and wife to become one flesh, polygamy was not intended and is therefore prohibited in the Christian congregation[25] - yet this extremely naive assertion has been challenged by Christian scholars themselves on the grounds that such a belief will implicate charges of:

> **'habitual fornication and adultery against the holy patriarchs and will also exclude from the sanctuary of God, the holy off springs which sprang from them - the entire nation of Israel - for it is said that a bastard shall not enter the**

---

[22] 1 Kings 11.1/32 Chronicles 11.213
[23] 2 Chronicles 11.21
[24] Apocryphal History of Joseph. vide. Farrar, Frederic W., The Life of Christ, p. 68
[25] Aid to Bible Understanding. Watch Tower Bible Society, p. 1116

**congregation of Jehovah even to the tenth
generation.'[26]**

Christ could not have declared polygamy non permissible in Christianity either through a clear commandment or even through implication since he is known to have declared quite categorically:

**'Think not that I have come to destroy the law or
the prophets: I am not come to destroy but fulfil.
For verily I say unto you, Till heavens and earth
pass, one jot or tittle shall in no wise pass from
the law, till all is fulfilled.'[27]**

The law to which Jesus referred with this declaration was doubtlessly the law expounded by the great Israelite law giver Moses which permitted the institution of polygamy within its Divine directives and therefore whatever was found permissible in the Law covenant had to be found permissible in any congregation which proposed to identify itself with Jesus. If Jesus is assumed to have required the faithful to abstain from polygamy altogether, then one would be obliged to admit that there is either a contradiction in his teachings or else he stood condemned for having taught people to break the eternal commandments of the law. One cannot however assume that he could have done this since he was quite insistent that:

**'Whosoever therefore shall break one of the least
of the commandments, and shall teach men so,
he shall be called the least in the kingdom of
heaven.'[28]**

---

[26] Milton, John
[27] Matthew 5.17/18
[28] Ibid 5.19

Hence, Christ could have not even remotely contemplated declaring polygamy as unlawful or else he would be considered the least in the kingdom of heaven and if he as much as dared annul this permissible injunctions of the Law covenant then he would have been himself guilty of gross misconduct. It is therefore fair to believe that whatever contradicts the requirement of the Mosaic Law in Christian teachings has to be a later innovation - an innovation contrary to the will and teaching of the person whose name is being used to further modern Christianity.

THE SERMON ON THE MOUNT

Some Christian schools of thought have often cited the Sermon on the Mount in evidence to argue that Christ outlawed polygamy when he declared:

> **'I say unto you, Whosoever shall put away his wife, except it be for fornication, and shall marry another, committeth adultery, and whoso marrieth her that is put away doth commit adultery.'[29]**

This passage when read in its proper perspective clearly establishes that it does not relate to the question of polygamy but to divorce. The background to the occasion when Christ uttered these words itself indicates that these words were necessitated as a consequence of Jesus's dialogue with the Pharisees which revolved around the question of divorce and not polygamy as evident from the Gospels of Matthew[30] and also Mark.[31]

Incidentally, at that particular point in time when Christ uttered these words, the Hillel and the Shammah schools of

---

[29] Ibid 19.9
[30] Ibid 19.3
[31] Mark 10.2

thought in Palestine differed on the permissibility of divorce in Hebrew law. The Hillel believed that a woman could be divorced by her husband for any reason whatsoever and therefore they argued that:

'a man might put away his wife for any cause because the son of Sirach saith if she not go as thou wouldst have her, cut her off from thy flesh, give her a bill of divorcement, and let her go.'[32]

The Shammah on the other hand believed that a wife could not be divorced except for adultery.[33] Therefore, either to resolve this issue or draw Christ in a snare, the Pharisees approached him:

'tempting him, and saying unto him, Is it lawful for a man to put away his wife for every cause?'[34]

In response to this query, Jesus referred to the original intent of Yahweh to the effect that the Lord had created a man and a woman in the beginning and therefore for this reason he should cleave to his wife since they are no longer two but one flesh and whatever God has joined together no man should put asunder.[35] He then stated that Moses had permitted them divorce because of the hardness of their hearts but it was not intended from the beginning[36]and therefore:

'Whosoever shall put away his wife, except it be for fornication, and shall marry another,

---

[32] Ecclus. 25/26
[33] Whitby. Illustrated National Family Bible, p. 940
[34] Matthew 19.3
[35] Ibid 19.4/6
[36] Ibid 19.7/8

> **committeth adultery; and whoso marrieth a her**
> **which is put away doth commit adultery.'[37]**

Christian scholars themselves admit that this dialogue between Jesus and the Pharisees ensued because the Pharisees suspected that Jesus's views did not conform to the Law of Moses and therefore they attempted to draw him in a snare. They state:

> **'The Pharisees had probably heard that Jesus opposed their decision concerning divorce and were desirous of drawing something from him which they could represent as contrary to the law of Moses. With this insidious design, they questioned whether it was lawful for a man to put away his wife for every cause, that is, on account of anything in her temper or person, or for any infirmity which rendered her disagreeable.'[38]**

It should therefore be evident that this passage from the Sermon on the Mount has absolutely no bearing whatsoever upon the question of polygamy. In fact, a closer examination of the passage itself suggests that polygamous marriages could be conducted within the permissible limits of the law provided the existing spouse is not divorced and subject to the man not denying his obligations to the estranged first wife since it appears from this passage that an essential ingredient for the second marriage to be considered unlawful would be for the man to put away his first wife for another. Otherwise, the passage maintains a unique silence in relation to the occasion where the man retains his first wife within a polygamous structure and continues to fulfil his obligations to

---

[37] Ibid 19.9
[38] Scott, Illustrated National Family Bible, p. 940

his estranged spouse as required by the laws in the Book of Exodus:

> **'If he take him another wife; her food, her raiment, and her duty of marriage, shall he not diminish.'[39]**

The specific inclusion of the requirement that a man 'put away his wife for another' before he is deemed to commit adultery indicates that the removal of the first spouse from the matrimonial scene is essential for the second marriage to be considered in breach of the law. But by virtue of retaining his first wife within a polygamous structure, a polygamous man's second marriage would fall outside the realm of the application of this law. Therefore it should logically follow that polygamy was found permissible by Christ and the Christian world has absolutely no cause whatsoever to make illegal of an institution which the Lord has made legal.

This argument is further substantiated when the law is applied separately to married men and married women. A close scrutiny of Christ's exposition of the law during his Sermon on the Mount reveals that a man who puts away his wife except for adultery and then proceeds to marry another is considered to have committed adultery.[40] The woman who has been put away is prohibited by the Christian law to engage into matrimony with another person during the lifetime of her husband who has put her away or else she shall be deemed to be an adulteress.[41] The law also discourages other men from engaging into a matrimonial contract with the woman who has been divorced and put away or else they too would be deemed to have committed adultery.[42]

---

[39] Exodus 21.10
[40] Matthew 19.9
[41] Romans 7.2/3
[42] Matthew 19.9

But the gospels and the epistles are totally silent in relation to the status of the second woman married by the husband after he has put away his first wife and this silence of the New Testament in branding the second wife as an adulterous woman also indicates that as far as her relationship with her husband is concerned, it is perfectly within the permissible limits of the law. This silence may in fact have been ingeniously devised by Christ to leave the fate of the first wife in imbalance until her husband realises the folly of his misdeed in putting her away and since the law has restricted her from marrying another man during the lifetime of her husband who has put her away for another women,[43] she would be free when he comes to his senses and therefore the prospects of her returning to his home within a polygamous structure would not have been hampered by her marriage to another person.

Several other passages of the New Testament lend support to this view. For instance, it has already been shown that while a polygamous marriage of a man has not been explicitly defined as adulterous unless he puts away his first wife - a married woman who is put away by her husband is positively required not to engage in matrimony with another man. If she fails to observe this law, her marriage is deemed to be adulterous on account of the following statement in the Epistles:

'For a woman which hath a husband is bound by the law to her husband so long as he liveth; but if the husband be dead, she is loosed from the law of her husband. So then if, while her husband liveth, she be married to another man, she shall be called an adulteress, though she be married to another man: but if her husband be

---

[43] Romans 7.2/3

dead, she is free from that law; so that she is no adulteress, though she be married to another man.44

This passage from the epistles of Paul places a positive restriction upon a woman engaging into polyandry since it denies her the right to marry another man within the lifetime of her husband while the Scriptures do not seem to place any positive restriction upon the conduct of a man. The gospels only state that a man who puts away his wife, that is, who divorces her except for adultery and then marries another commits adultery. The silence of the Scriptures to govern the conduct of a man with a similar kind of a restriction as in relation to the conduct of a woman who is not permitted to marry at all within the lifetime of her husband who puts her away supports the argument that polygamy was considered perfectly permissible in Christian teachings.

POLYGAMY AND PAUL'S EPISTLES

The abolition of polygamy in the Christian congregation is also argued on the strength of certain passages contained in Paul's epistles to Timothy, the first bishop of the Church of Ephesians and Titus, the bishop of the Church of Cretians. In the first instance, these two epistles which allegedly contain passages restricting polygamy are universally accepted to be pastoral epistles[45] and as such do not concern the Christian laity since Paul is believed to have written these to:

'show very particularly what manner of persons the bishops and elders ordained into the ministry of Christ ought to be so that ambition and improper desires after the sacred service might

---

[44] Ibid
[45] Eddie, John. Illustrated National Family Bible, p. 1145

> **be repressed and those that are appointed to it might know how to behave in it.'[46]**

Christian authorities also admit that Paul's epistles to Timothy and Titus on the basis of which this alleged non permissibility of polygamy is generally argued were written by him to brief his agents about what kind of:

> **'tenderness, holiness, vigilance, fidelity and zeal ought to characterise the people ordained into the service of the Church.'[47]**

It is therefore incorrect to assume that the rules and regulations which concerned the Christian clergy applied universally to the entire Christian laity since one does not find any mention of Christian laymen in these passages of Paul's epistles which are allegedly stated to contain a restriction on polygamy.

ESSENCE OF PAUL'S ADVISE

The subject matter of Paul's directives in his epistles to Timothy[48] and Titus[49] on the basis of which polygamy is argued to have been allegedly forbidden in Christianity indicate that these related to the prospective candidates to the ministry of the Church and not the general public. This is indicated by the mention of the office of bishops[50] and deacons[51] in Paul's first epistle to Timothy as well as elders[52] and bishops or overseers[53] in his epistle to Titus. Since these people were expected to be counsellors to the Christian congregation, their conduct and character was bound to

---

[46] Scott. Illustrated National Family Bible, 1147
[47] Eddie. Illustrated National Family Bible, p. 1145
[48] 1 Timothy 3.1/15
[49] Titus 1.5/11
[50] 1 Timothy 3.1
[51] Ibid 3.8 & 12
[52] Titus 1.5
[53] Ibid 1.7

influence the spiritual as well as moral and material welfare of their congregation and unless these people themselves knew how to be behave properly, they could not be expected to reform the Christians laymen under their charge. It was for this reason that Paul directed Timothy and Titus to be particularly careful with the choice of the ministers selected to oversee the welfare of their respective congregations. Hence, with these epistles, Paul was setting forth the guidelines and minimum standards for prospective candidates desirous to be ordained to the ministry of the Church and amongst this long list of qualifications he stipulated to Titus:

> 'For this cause left I thee in Crete, that thou shouldst set in order the things that are wanting, and ordain elders in every city, as I had appointed thee: If any be blameless, the husband of one wife, having faithful children, not accused of riot, or unruly. For the bishop must be blameless, as the steward of God; not self willed, not soon angry, not given to wine, no striker, not given to filthy lucre; But a lover of hospitality, a lover of good men, sober, just, holy temperate; Holding fast the faithful word as he hath been taught, that he may be able by sound doctrine both to exhort and to convince the gainsayers. For there are many unruly and vain talkers and deceivers, specially they of the circumcision: Whose mouths must be stopped; who subvert whole houses, teaching things which they ought not, for filthy lucre's sake.'[54]

In a similar directive to Timothy, the first bishop appointed unto the Ephesians, Paul sent the instructions:

---

[54] Titus 1.5/11

'If a man desire the office of a bishop, he desireth a good work. A bishop the must be blameless, the husband of one wife, vigilant, sober, of good behaviour, given to hospitality, apt to teach: Not given to wine, no striker, nor greedy of filthy lucre; but patient, not a brawler, not covetous: One that ruleth his house, having his children in subjection with all gravity; For if a man know not how to rule his own house, how shall he take care of the church of God? Not a novice, lest being lifted with pride, he fall into the condemnation of the devil. Moreover, he must have a good report of them which are without; lest he fall into reproach and the snare of the devil. Likewise must the deacons be grave, not double tongued, not given to much wine, not greedy of filthy lucre; Holding the mystery of faith in a pure conscience. And let these also first be proved; then let them use the office of the deacon, being found blameless. Even so must their wives be grave, not slanderers, sober, faithful in all things. Let the deacons be the husbands of one wife, ruling their children and their houses well. For they that have used the office of the deacon well purchase for themselves a good degree, and great boldness in the faith which is in Christ Jesus.'[55]

These passage should establish beyond a shadow of doubt the fact that the directives contained within these epistles were exclusively addressed to the Christian clergy only or the prospective candidates to the ministry of the Church. It is therefore grossly incorrect to apply this rule concerning *one wife* to the laity and consequently outlaw the long established

---

[55] 1 Timothy 3.1/13

institution of polygamy in Christianity - an institution found perfectly permissible in Biblical law which Christ himself admitted was eternal and of which not one jot or tittle was to pass till heaven and earth pass.[56]

In addition to this, one observes that the determiner *one* used in the context of these passages, particularly in Paul's epistle to Timothy[57] is not used as a determiner of quantity otherwise the entire passage would be grammatically incorrect and Paul would be considered to be suggesting that 'all deacons should be the husbands of one wife' - that is, married to one single woman.

A POSITIVE REQUIREMENT

A minute scrutiny of these passages indicates that these directives rather than placing prohibitive conditions on the Christian clergy, demanded a positive requirement in so much that appointees to responsible offices in the Christian church ought not be single persons or novices but married men - husbands and fathers so that they are seen to be persons who rule their households well and who hold their families in subjection. This is clearly indicated by the passage:

> **'For if a man not know how to rule his own house, how shall he take care of the church of God.'[58]**

A novice being a person new to any field of activity - in the context of these passage a person who is not familiar with the extremely complex and intricate subject of handling people under one's authority could not be expected to fulfil

---

[56] Matthew 5.18
[57] 1 Timothy 3.12
[58] 1 Timothy 3.5

his duties satisfactorily. This fact is admitted by Christian scholars also who state that:

'It is only in a married state that some of the purest, most disinterested, and most elevated principles of our nature are called into exercise. All that concerns filial piety and paternal and especially material affection depends on marriage for its very existence. It is in the bosom of the family that there is constant call for all acts of kindness, or self denial or forbearance and of love. The family therefore is the sphere best applied for the development of all social virtues.'[59]

Paul's insistence that only married men be ordained into the clergy and not novices was motivated by the realisation of the responsibility entrusted upon the leaders of the congregation - the elders who were required to help their parishioners in all aspects of their lives including domestic and matrimonial affairs. They were expected to accustom their congregation on how to conduct their domestic lives in accordance with the requirements of their faith and advise them on how to attend to their affairs with their wives and children in a thoroughly Christian manner as expounded by Paul. They were also supposed to counsel their flock on how to live in a marriage without contravening the covenants of the law.

It cannot be denied that these Church leaders were bound to be looked upon by the laity to solve the domestic, marital and conjugal problems experienced by the members of their parish and unless these guardians of the fold were themselves accustomed to the practicality of domestic and matrimonial life they could not be expected to be pragmatic in their advice nor in their approach to the problems of their

---

[59] Hodge, Dr. Charles. Systematic Theology, vol. iii, p. 371

parishioners. Therefore Paul insisted that the people who become guardians of the Christian laity and consequently the Church itself should be men experienced in handling their own families in a proper manner which could not be expected of a novice on account of his lack of experience in these matters. This fact is once again admitted by Christian scholars who state:

'**They could no better teach or counsel people about marriage than the paint salesman can advise the artist or the stone cutter advice the sculptor. The blind cannot teach art. Those born deaf cannot conduct symphonies.**'[60]

PRECAUTIONARY MEASURE

The ministers of the Church, besides being entrusted with grave responsibility of their parish were also placed in an exceptional position of trust and Paul was not unaware of the temptations which could be occasioned by a clergyman during the course of his duties as a spiritual guide, marriage counsellor, psychologist, family physician and advisor on several other matters affecting the spiritual, ethical, moral and other physical aspects of his parishioners -men as well as women whether young or old and also pious or otherwise. However, in view of the fallible nature of a man believed by Paul to have been born a sinner, Paul demanded that the ministers of the Church be men of high integrity as well as means and experience lest they fall into the condemnation of the devil.[61] Since a married man with a wife, if sincere to his trust was more apt to avoid the snare of the devil and consequently any kind of a physical temptation he being in a better position to lawfully exercise his natural sexual drives

---

[60] McLoughlin, Emmett. People's Padre
[61] 1 Timothy 3.7

171

and also since being a husband he was in a better position to understand the sanctity of marriage, Paul insisted that the clergymen appointed to these exceptionally responsible positions of trust be married men.

In fact, Biblical scholars have themselves laid a particularly heavy stress upon the character of the ministers of the Church while commenting upon these passages in the epistles of Paul. They have argued that whatever natural abilities one possessed 'he might be considered ineligible to this office of trust if he was not of blameless character and not avoided scandalous vices.'[62] In insisting that the minister's be a married man, Paul himself avoided the probability of future scandal in the Church and hence reproach by those that are not a part of the Christian congregation[63] and the wisdom of Paul's precautionary measures in enlisting married men only into the ministry of the Church has more often than not been proved by subsequent events in Christian history. For instance, the study of imposed celibacy in some Christian churches is admitted to have been:

'made a cause of scandal and shame to the Christian church. It has had the effect of belittling the sanctity of marriage relation and sapped all the vigour of manhood from those who must employ the continual force of the mind and will against the natural body urge. Its victims have confessed that far from freeing them from sexual urges, it has actually bred a very ferment of impurity of mind.'[64]

The practical effects of this induced unnatural law which deprives clergymen from exercising their natural physical desires in a lawful and permissible manner and which Paul

---

[62] Scott. Illustrated national Family Bible, p. 1147
[63] 1 Timothy 3.7
[64] Lehmann, L.H. The Soul of a Priest

proposed to avoid have been experienced extensively in the history of the Christian church. It is admitted that

'no priest who has heard the priests confession and has any respect for truth will deny that sexual affairs are extremely common among the clergy.'[65]

It has also been stated that the denial of the legality of marriage enforced upon the members of the clergy has resulted in 'the custom of clerical concubines with resultant generations of illegitimate offspring'[66] and that many a clergymen are known to have 'become addicts to debauchery and all sorts of vile abominations, even unnatural sin'[67] to the extent that 'an Italian bishop of the tenth century described the morals of his time saying that if he were to enforce the canons against unchaste persons administering ecclesiastical rites, no one would be left in the church except the boys.'[68]

These claims may sound exaggerated to a layman but the truth is that such Church organisations which choose to impose celibacy upon its clergy in thorough disregard of Paul's demand that members of clergy be married men only have found themselves heavily burden with sexual immorality even to the highest position in the Church hierarchy. Pope John XI for instance is stated to have been the illegitimate son of Pope Sergius III while Pope John XII is declared to have been such a thoroughly immoral man that the people of Rome complained of his debaucheries and he was finally tried for, amongst other things, adultery and incest. Pope Alexander VI is also stated to have fathered six illegitimate children, two of which were born after he became the pontiff and Pope John

---

[65] McLoughlin, Emmett. People's Padre
[66] Lehmann, L.H. Out of the Labyrinth
[67] Demetrius, T. Catholicism and Protestantism
[68] Lecky, William E.H. History of European Morals

XXIII is believed to have been deposed because of his immorality.[69]

It is exactly this kind of moral laxity which Paul's directives mistakenly construed to have banned polygamy in the Christian congregation proposed to avoid. With his clear instructions that potential clergymen should be married men and not bachelors or novices who could easily fall into the temptations of lusty flesh, Paul wished to avoid the situation where these guardians of the Church could not only fall into transgression themselves but also tempted innocent parishioners into sin. This fear of moral laxity within the holy Christian order was Paul's main preoccupation while writing these epistles to Timothy and Titus since to:

'deprive the Church of honourable marriage was to fill her with concubines, incest, and all manner of nameless vice and uncleanliness.'[70]

In his epistle to Timothy which Christian clergymen have construed to be a prohibition of polygamy, Paul is also seen to advise Timothy to ensure that he treated 'elder women as mothers and younger as sisters with all purity' but he denied women under the age of sixty access to the service of the Church and instead demanded that the services of younger widows be refused and they be advised to marry and bear children so that the adversaries of the Church may not have an occasion to speak reproachfully.[71] It is therefore evident from the scrutiny of these passages in Paul's epistles that his purpose in issuing these directives had no relation whatsoever to the question of polygamy. His only concern was to discourage all avenues which could lead to the ministers of the Church into temptation and consequently the ministry into scandal and contempt. By insisting that the officials of the

---

[69] Boettner, Loraine. Roman Catholicism
[70] Bernard of Clairvaux
[71] 1 Timothy 5.2/14

Church be married men or else women of mature age, Paul hoped to keep the administration of the Church beyond reproach.

The absence of the prenominal adjective *only* within the context of the original manuscripts where Paul issues the directives that the clergymen ought to be husbands of *one wife* also suggests that his purpose was not to restrict polygamy to the clergy but the clergy to celibate persons. Had these directives related to polygamy then the prenominal adjective would have positively been added to the text and therefore the passages would have read something like 'the husbands of only one wife.' Nevertheless, as these directives stand at present, the only message which one may decode from these is that the state of matrimony was a prerequisite to the ministry of Christ and not as is mistakenly assumed - a universal prohibition of the long established and permissible institution of polygamy.

ADDRESSED TO CLERGY ONLY

Nevertheless, if it is still insisted that these passages positively deal with polygamy, then one need appreciate that these were addressed exclusively to the elders of the Christian church - to the bishops and elders and deacons and overseers. Therefore, if there are any restrictions imposed upon polygamy by these directives then these are imposed upon such persons as aspire to serve the Church in some official capacity and hence ought to be confined to the Christian clergy and not extended to the laity.

Christian scholars have often argued that because the over-seers and ministerial servants of the church are supposed to set an example for the rest of the congregation, a limitation imposed upon them may safely be extended to ordinary men of the Church. While one admits that the leaders in every society are expected to set an example for the laymen to follow, yet if this line of argument was accepted in this instance then one would assume that the most excellent example for the Christians to follow would be that of the highest of the high priests in the Christian congregation - Jesus Christ who remained, so it is stated, totally celibate throughout his earthly life. Nevertheless, there is absolutely no credible evidence in the New Testament itself to assume that either Christ or Paul denied the Christian congregation the right to continue this long established and permissible institution of polygamy since in neither of these Biblical passages often referred to by Christians do either Jesus or Paul refer to the subject of polygamy nor do they concern themselves with it. In fact, Christian scholars who argue against the permissibility of polygamy on the basis of these epistles of Paul themselves admit that while Christ and the apostles allegedly:

> **'condemned polygamy, as well as divorces, except for adultery; yet there was no direct command for man, who had previously taken more wives than one, to put the others away when they embraced the gospel.'[72]**

It has already been shown that the Biblical passages on the basis of which this institution is alleged stated to have been positively condemned by Christ or the apostles, rather Paul, have no bearing on the question of polygamy whatsoever since these either concern divorce or else the question of eligibility to the order of Christian clergy. On the other hand, the mere fact that there 'was no direct command for a polygamous man to put away his wives, other than one,' indicates that polygamy was considered a permissible institution within the realm of the Judaeo-Christian law -

---

[72] Scott. Illustrated National Family Bible

unless it is to be stated that Christ or the apostles disregarded the express will of Yahweh.

Furthermore, if it was accepted that these passages in the synoptic gospels or the epistles did positively abolish polygamy then the Christian masses would be obliged to admit that both Christ and Paul would be deemed to have destroyed the law and therefore considered 'the least in the kingdom of heaven for having taught the masses to break one of the commandments of the law - the law of which not one jot or tittle was to pass till heaven and earth did pass.'[73]

HISTORY OF THE CHRISTIAN NATIONS

The subsequent history of the Christian nations and also the conduct and pronouncements of its leaders and elders bears evidence that they not only found polygamy permissible within Christianity but it was also widely practised with full sanction of the Church. Saint Augustine, one of the most renowned and respected Church fathers admitted the legality of polygamy while the great German leader of the Protestant reformation, Martin Luther acknowledged its permissibility under certain conditions. The 17th century anti Episcopalian refused to subscribe to the view of the anti-polygamy lobby 'lest by implication, the holy patriarchs and the pillars of faith who had more than one wife be charged of habitual fornication and adultery.' Milton was of the opinion that if the permissibility of polygamy was denied then one would be 'forced to exclude from the sanctuary of God as spurious, the holy offspring which sprang from them - yea, all the sons of Israel for whom the sanctuary was itself made for it is said that a bastard shall not enter the congregation of the Lord even to his tenth generation.'

---

[73] Matthew 5.18/19

History also records that amongst others, such faithful sons of the Church as Charlemagne, the Frankish leader decorated with the title of the Protector of the Church and also Diarmait, the 16th century king of Ireland or Fredrick of Prussia and Phillip of Hesse were all polygamous men. In fact, western sociologists have themselves acknowledged that:

'although under public ban and also branded as immoral by official public opinion, nevertheless there is undisputable evidence that polygamy is now practised by thousands of people throughout Europe.'[74]

In modern times also, the leader of the Church of Jesus Christ of Latter Day Saints, Joseph Smith of the Mormon fame judged in favour of the institution as have many other intelligent Christian advocated polygamy. Hence, these evidences should establish the permissibility of polygamy in Christianity.

POLYGAMY AND ISLAM

When Islam first made its appearance in Arabia, polygamy was found to be a legitimate institution in most pre-Islamic cultures and religions. Nonetheless, its permissibility was being abused extensively to an extent where it beneficence to mankind was being sacrificed at the altar of physical lust and greed. In Arabia itself, polygamy was widely practised by the Arabs whose harems were often further expanded on the deaths of their fathers since it was an accepted convention amongst the Arabs to inherited not only the estates of their deceased fathers but also their step mothers which they normally took into their own harems.[75]

---

[74] Field, Allen. Digest Review, 1946
[75] Sahih Bukhari 85.6

Although Islam, like all other faiths and cultures accepted the practical necessity of this essential institution yet unlike other religions it did not encourage its practical implementation except under the most demanding circumstances. It appears that Islam remained totally silent on the question of polygamy till after the Battle of Uhud when the small Muslim community at Medina suffered heavy losses and nearly ten percent of its male population was slain in the battlefield. This unfortunate decimation of a large proportion of Muslim men left behind it a large number of orphans, widows and surplus women and therefore it was proper that the Quran should address this social problem and offer a solution to it which it did with the revelation of the following passage:

'O mankind, be mindful of your duty to your Lord, Who created you from a single soul and of its kind created its mate, and from them twain spread many men and women: and be mindful of your duty to Allah, in Whose name you appeal to one another, and of your obligations in respect of ties of kinship. Verily Allah watches over you. And give to the orphans their property and exchange not the bad for the good, and devour not their property by mixing it with your own. Surely, this is a great sin. And if you fear that you will not be fair in dealing with the orphans, then marry of women as may be agreeable to you, two or three or four: and if you fear you will not deal justly, then marry only one or what your right hand possess. This is the nearest way for you to avoid injustice.'[76]

---

[76] Al Quran 4.2/4

PROTECTION OF ORPHANS AND UNPROTECTED FEMALES

It is to be observed here that this passage of the Quran which permits polygamy in Islam was revealed to Prophet Muhammad[sa] while the question of orphans in the society was being addressed by God Almighty and Muslims were being exhorted to protect their rights and interests.[77] It should therefore be evident that this institution has been permitted in Islam to principally address the question of the welfare of these unfortunate victims of fate weakened by the loss of their natural guardians and protectors - weakened to the extent that if left unprotected to the mercy of circumstances, they were extremely likely to suffer severe handicap and hardship. But since Islam was extremely aware of the need to protect the interest of this weak and unprotected section of its society and also provide secure and stable homes for them, the Quran exhorted Muslims to marry from amongst them considering that their rights could be better protected within the structure of a secure household. Hence, permission to resort to polygamy in Islam was given with a view to solve an extremely urgent and delicate problem and its purpose was to provide protection to the orphans and also protect their interests and not to satiate any kind of physical lust.

This fact is also evident from an extension to this Quranic passage which states:

> 'They seek directions from thee in the matter of marrying more women than one. Say to them: Allah has given you directions concerning them. The commandment given to you elsewhere in the Book has reference to orphan girls whom you give not what is prescribed for them and yet

---

[77] Ibid 4.3

whom you desire to marry, and to unprotected female children. You have also been commanded to deal equitably with orphans. Whatever good you do, Allah knows it well.[78]

However, aware that human nature was weak and hence prone to be unjust, the Quran counselled Muslims not to marry from amongst the orphans if they feared that they may not be able to do justice to them since the very purpose of the permissibility of polygamy would otherwise be defeated. Instead, it advised them to marry from amongst the other women as may seem agreeable to them[79] but since this advice was itself being given in consideration of the circumstances being faced by the society, it was not to be deemed a licence to abuse the permissibility of this essential and honourable institution.

MEANS TO COMPENSATE FOR DEPLETED MALE POPULATION

It is worthy of note that Islam imposed a responsibility upon Muslims to arrange marriages of the widows and slaves amongst them[80] and also female captives taken in the course of war[81] and these passages of the Quran are stated to have been revealed at Medina by which time Muslims had suffered severe depletion of its already small male population on account of several battles and military expeditions forced upon them by their adversaries. Consequently, it would not have been possible for Muslims to fulfil these obligation imposed upon them by God Almighty unless they were permitted polygamy. Hence, every evidence indicates that the

---

[78] Al Quran 4.128
[79] Ibid 4.4
[80] Ibid 24.33
[81] Ibid 4.4

primary reason for which Islam permitted this institution was to provide eligible husbands for the orphans and widows as well as slaves and captives of war in its society which had suffered severe preponderance of females over males on account of the wars imposed upon it by its enemies.

The effects of human strife has always borne a heavy burden upon mankind throughout its history with the severe depletion of the male species and surplus of women in a society and in such situations the only sensible course of action has been to encourage polygamy as for instance was done in 1650 when after a thirty year war, certain Christian sects advocated polygamy and consequently the Frankish king Kriestag passed a resolution at Nuremberg stating that:

> **'henceforth every man should be allowed to marry two women."[82]**

The wisdom of such action has been acknowledged by western intellectuals themselves who state that it is thoroughly unfair to deprive women a right to exercise their perfectly natural desires merely on account of the arithmetical scarcity of men in their society. It is for instance admitted that:

> **'in all countries where there is an excess of women, it is an obvious injustice that those women who by arithmetical necessity must remain unmarried should be wholly debarred from sexual experience.'[83]**

The practical effects of the more recent global wars within nearly two decades of each other has been felt closely by our own generation during the present century due to the severe

---

[82] History of Human Marriages, vol. iii
[83] Russell, Bertrand. Marriage and Morals, p. 47

decimation of the male population. It is for instance been admitted that in the wake of the:

'First World War, casualties and other factors resulted in an enormous surplus of women throughout Europe. The excess of women in France, Italy and Germany was well over twenty percent while in Russia it was thirty two percent and in Poland nearly thirty eight percent.'[84]

This high ratio of the surviving female population in the wake of only one global war brought down with it added problems to the world which had already suffered severe hardship and deprivation on account of the extended strife. As husbands and eligible bachelors failed to return from the battlefields where they lost their lives, widows at home on both sides of the warring factions were forced to lead solitary lives without the soothing companionship of their departed husbands and orphans were deprived of the strength of their fathers while women of marriageable age were forced to compete against others in a highly competitive environment on account of the shortage of sufficient prospective husbands.

DESTRUCTION OF MORAL VALUES

This sad situation was further aggravated by the surviving men who, finding themselves a rare commodity took full advantage of their abstinence on the war front and made themselves available to as many women as they possibly could while women, unable to assuage their perfectly natural physical drives in a matrimonial environment permitted them to take full advantage of the situation which eventually began to erode the moral standards of the suffering nations to the

---

[84] Scheinfield, Amran. Shortage of Husbands

extent that in our present age morality has come to be considered an ancient weakness.

The deplorable after effects of this moral laxity occasioned by the two global wars is being increasingly suffered by the western world in several ways - as for instance in the increase of sexually transmitted disease which has been on a steep rise since the two wars. It is reported that in the United States alone, Chlamydia, a sexually transmitted venereal disease infects as many as 3,000,000 Americans an year. Official statistics also indicate that between 1969 and 1981, venereal disease among only American students increased from 1% to 16.8%. This is despite an admission that almost 90% of cases involving such diseases as syphilis are not reported.[85] In Denmark, the rate of reported increase in venereal disease is as high as 250% amongst persons between 16 to 20 and 400% in persons of 15 and under and in the United Kingdom itself, latest figures released by the Department of Health indicate that in England alone, the number of new cases of Genito Urinary diseases seen every year has increased to as much as 600,000 thus registering an increase of some 27,772 over the previous year[86] and this experience is shared by most predominantly Christian countries of the west.

In permitting polygamy within limitations, Islam has designed a system of contingency to supply eligible husbands in times of severe shortage and also provide a safeguard to preserve the chastity of both sexes as well as protect the moral virtues of a society but societies which deny polygamy as a safety valve by enforcing a rigid system of monogamy have been seen to have been ripped apart with total destruction of moral values - a fact admitted by western writers who compliment Islam for its wisdom of permitting this essential institution. For instance, they state:

---

[85] Readers Digest, July 1964
[86] Department of Health, Summary Information SM12B

'In the west, there is pretended monogamy but
real polygamy without responsibility. The
mistress is cast off when the man becomes weary
of her and she sinks gradually into a woman of
the street because her former lover has no
responsibility for her future and she is far worse
off than a sheltered wife and the mother in a
polygamous home. When we see thousands of
miserable women crowd the streets of western
towns at night, we must surely feel that it does
not lie in the western mouths to reproach Islam
for its polygamy.'[87]

This western thinker and sociologist, herself a woman, then
proceeds to state that:

'It is better for a woman, happier for her and
more respectable to be consorted to one man
only with a legitimate child in her arms and
surrounded with respect than to be seduced and
cast out in the street perhaps with an
illegitimate child outside the pale of law -
unsheltered and uncared for, to become a victim
of any passer by, night after night, rendered
incapable of motherhood -despised.'[88]

Another extremely deplorable result of this severe depletion
of male population has been the extra responsibility imposed
upon women to tend for their families and provide them with
basic sustenance and necessities of life. Hence they were
forced to leave their principal responsibility at home to earn a
living at the cost of the welfare of their children who were
deserted while mothers went out to grind the mill and

---

[87] Besant, Andie. vide: Maulana Abdul Majid Daryabandi,
Translation and Commentary of the Holy Quran, pp. 146/47
[88] Ibid

consequently children brought up without proper parental supervision at home took to the streets and the entire structure of the family began to break down. In 1981 for instance, England and Wales registered a staggering 81,666 illegitimate births and 128,581 legal abortions of which 26,430 unwanted pregnancies were terminated by teenagers. In 1982, this figure increased to 163,045 of which 93,290 pregnancies were terminated by single women and 16,453 by widows, divorcees or separated women. This figure registered a further increase in 1991 with 167,376 legal abortion of which 110,879 pregnancies were terminated by single women and 3,158 by children under 16 while 31,130 were by teenagers between the ages of 16 and 19.

The figure for the dissolutions of marriages on ground of adultery in England and Wales alone, as much as 48,013 of the total number of 173,452 in 1981 also indicates the extent to which family life has suffered in the western societies.

These figures are doubtlessly a direct result of the loss of moral standards occasioned as an aftermath of the two global wars and this state of affairs could have been avoided to a great extent had the western nations considered the merits of polygamy since it could have provided homes to many of these war widows and maidens of marriageable age and consequently given them an opportunity to fulfil their perfectly natural and legitimate physical needs without having to resort to covert actions - a fact admitted by western sociologists of repute who state that:

'A return to polygamy, that natural relationship between the sexes would remedy many evils; prostitution, venereal disease, abortion, the misery of illegitimate children, the misfortune of millions of unmarried women resulting from

disproportion between sexes, adultery and even jealousy.[89]

The institution of polygamy in Islam was principally intended to meet such serious situations that follow in the wake of a war when the male population of a nation is depleted to an extent that it begins to threaten the moral fibre of a society with destruction and the preponderance of women over men begins to lead a nation into social and moral degeneration and while the Christian world may not be prepared to accept the wisdom of permitting this institution yet it looks upon the Islamic civilization with envy as for instance one observes from the comments of a leading English clergyman who stated at a Church Congress held in London:

'Owing to polygamy, Muslim countries are free from professional outcasts, a greater reproach to Christendom than polygamy is to Islam. The strictly regulated polygamy of the Muslim lands is infinitely less degrading to women and less injurious to men than the promiscuous polyandry which is the curse of the Christian cities and which is absolutely unknown in Islam.'[90]

A SACRIFICIAL INSTITUTION

The institution of polygamy in Islam is therefore designed to meet such challenges and exigencies of life. It is an institution permitted by Divine decree to elevate suffering and when practised within the legal and permissible limits of Quranic injunctions, it is not only justifiable but also commendable as

---

[89] Bon, Dr. Le. vide: Polygamy, Islami Mission, Lahore
[90] Taylor, Rev. Isaac. vide: Maulana Abdul Majid Daryabandi, Translation and Commentary of the Holy Quran, p. 569

an act of charity since it was designed for the noble purpose of providing relief to the unfortunate victims of fate in a society and also offer a home to the widows and their orphaned children who on account of their new family ties do not remain strangers in the household of their new husbands or step fathers but became members of the household.

Polygamy has no doubt been often condemned as an institution which proposes to find means of sexual gratification but in essence it constitutes a great sacrifice - a sacrifice demanded of both men and women in which personal sentiments are required to be subordinated to the wider communal and national interests. It imposes a heavy burden upon the resources of a man who is not only required to take under his protection an additional wife but also assume responsibility of her deceased husband's orphaned children. He is expected to provide for their basic needs of food, clothing and housing as well as education and in eastern cultures, particularly where regional customs still persist and respect for Islamic law is rather slack in comparison to cultural traditions, men who take in their custody orphaned daughters of their secondary wives often find themselves in a heavy financial burden when these girls become of marriageable age and suitable husbands are to be sought for them. Yet, Muslims who engage in polygamy as an act of charity bear this burden cheerfully, irrespective of the heavy burden imposed upon them. They accept their responsibility and cope with the situation in the best possible manner relying upon the succour of God to assist them in their honourable duty.

In addition to these material demands, a polygamous man is also required to carry a very heavy psychological burden. He is expected to treat all his wives with equality and justice and Islam demands that he treat his own children as well as the children of his wives from their former husbands with the same affection and love which in a confined and possibly an overcrowded environment may not be an easy task since such an extension of one's household could easily lead to a certain amount of physical discomfort and also acute jealousy and resentment which a polygamous man is required to cope with and endure.

Women in a polygamous structure are also expected to forego some of their most cherished rights for the greater welfare of the society. They are required to tighten their budgets and possibly forego some luxuries to which they may be accustomed and the privacy of their homes is invaded by the additional wives of their husbands and their children who begin to demand and exercise equal rights upon it. They are also obliged to share their most cherished possession - their husbands with other women and so are the children in a polygamous household expected to share their privileges, their homes and their parents with strangers whom Islam grants equitable rights in the household of their step fathers.

But all these sacrifices are made to serve the community at large and it is rather ironic that while the Christian faith appears to be extremely rich in words in so much that it states that 'pure religion, and undefiled, before God and the Father, is to visit the fatherless and the widows in their affliction'[91] yet it denies these orphans and widows the strength and security of domestic lives even under circumstances where polygamy is probably the only answer to the society's problems. Alas, were the Christian nations who prohibit polygamy be wiser to the wisdom contained in their scriptures:

'Wilt thou know, O vain man, that faith without works is dead.'[92] For as the body without the

---

[91] James 1.27
[92] James 2.20

spirit is dead, so faith without works is also dead.'93

MULTIPLICATION OF HUMAN SPECIES

Polygamy in Islam is not a licence for a man to multiply the number of his wives at will but an obligation to cope with numerous urgent situations which demand attention and which for the greater welfare of the society cannot be ignored. As a general rule, every Divine religion has recognised the union of one man and one woman as a valid form of marriage but it has been observed that in some exceptional circumstances all religions have permitted man to marry more than one wife and Islam itself is not an exception to this rule.

The multiplication of the human species has been stated to be the Divine design of the Lord who required Adam and Eve to be fruitful[94] and marriage is stated to have been ordained as the proper arrangement to realise and accomplish this Divine purpose. Yet, certain unforeseeable conditions may prevail in a marriage where the very purpose of this Divine union may be defeated by circumstances beyond the control of individuals. A woman could for instance be found incapable of conception and unless polygamous marriages were found permissible, the only resort a man who desired an heir would have would be to divorce his barren or ailing wife and marry another which could render the already suffering spouse homeless with no future prospects of marriage on account of her inability to conceive a seed and thus provide her husband with an heir. However, polygamy opens legitimate avenues

---

[93] Ibid 2.26
[94] Genesis 1.28

for the man to realise his dream while retaining his barren or ailing wife within a polygamous structure.

LAXITY OF MORALS

In other circumstances, conditions could also prevail where a wife could be suffering from such permanent disorder as to render her incapable of fulfilling her physical duties in marriage and hence a husband could be forced to lead a life of abstinence or else take recourse to either of the two most detestable options, adultery or divorce. But, the first of these three options defeats the very purpose of marriage[95] while the second has not only been condemned as a manifest sin[96] which eats into the vitals of a civilized society and brings a person's soul to ruin[97] but it has also been described as a sin against God.[98] The third detestable option of divorce renders women homeless with little prospect of their being able to find a secure matrimonial home on account of their inability to bear children. Hence, the only sane course to follow under these unfortunate circumstances would be for man to wed another wife while still retaining his ailing spouse in a polygamous structure and the wisdom of this course of action has been admitted by the Judaeo-Christian leaders also as for instance in an edict issued by the Roman Catholic Church in 726 CE, Pope Gregory II stated that:

> 'if a wife is attacked with a malady which renders her unfit for conjugal relations, the husband may marry another but in that case he must allow his sick wife all kinds of necessary support and assistance.'

---

[95] Genesis 1.28
[96] Al Quran 17.33
[97] Proverbs 6.32/33
[98] Genesis 39.9

Such a course of action is in fact the only sane course which a person could follow and which offers the best security to those unfortunate women who find themselves barren or suffering from such ailments which render them incapable of fulfilling their roles as mothers to their children and wives to their husbands. It can also not be denied that under these conditions women would be better placed to live in safety and security in a polygamous household rather than be turned out in the cold and be forsaken by their husbands since:

'The woman's natural jealousy is not in a man loving another but at his forsaking him.'[99]

One could no doubt argue that both these reasons for which polygamy is considered the only correct course displays a certain amount of bias against women in so much that it is quite possible for the situation to be revered and a husband, rather than the wife is either infertile or stricken with an ailment which renders him incapable of fathering children or else fulfilling his duties in a marriage. Nonetheless, in the first instance it is an admitted psychological fact that women have always proved to be emotionally more rational and understanding in their outlook and therefore better endowed by nature to accept the misfortunes of their lives and also the shortcoming of others in a more charitable manner than men have ever proved to be on account of their emotional weakness. While both sexes contain within themselves a natural and legitimate desire to have children, women have always been seen to be better geared to accept the inevitable when their husbands are infertile - even in the most allegedly emancipated societies of the west. Their superior sense of loyalty to their husbands has, as a rule rather than an exception been instrumental in the survival of their marriages under such unfortunate circumstances while men do not by

---

[99] Toynbee. vide: Polygamy, Islami Mission

nature reconcile easily if their desire to have an issue to succeed them and perpetuate their name is frustrated.

On the other hand, it is once again an acknowledged fact that a women are better endowed to control their natural physical instincts while the sexual instincts of men are probably the most powerful of all their natural physical instincts and it is certainly much more difficult for them to channel their energy in other spheres. Nevertheless, if a woman is not prepared to accept such an unfortunate situation in her life then although Islam considers divorce to be a detestable thing[100] yet it does not permit its prejudices to stand in her way nor does it deprive her the right to exercise her natural and perfectly legitimate faculties since it gives her an absolute right to divorce her husband and marry another.[101] Although a sad option, yet, the only other alternative would be to permit polyandry which Islam does not permit for some very valid reasons.

A CAUTIOUS INJUNCTION

The institution of polygamy has therefore been permitted in Islam principally to address the question of orphans[102] and other unprotected women[103] and also provide a remedy to many other social and moral problems which may arise in a society and which may not be possible to solve in a monogamous society. However despite its permissibility under such compelling and urgent conditions, Islam approaches the entire question of polygamy with extreme caution and admonishes Muslims:

---

[100] Sunan Abu Daud
[101] Sahih Bukhari 63.4
[102] Al Quran 4.4
[103] Ibid 4.128

'If you fear that you will not be able to do justice, the marry only one or what your right hand possess. That is the nearest way for you to obviate injustice.'[104]

The fact that it is not humanly possible for a man to keep a perfect emotional balance between his wives in a polygamous is also not overlooked nor denied by Islam and the Quran states quite clearly that:

'You cannot keep perfect balance between your wives, however much you may desire it.'[105]

These passage of the Quran should therefore indicate that polygamy is not to be resorted to lightly since it imposes a heavy burden upon polygamous men in nearly every sphere of their lives including such aspects upon which one may not have control, such as feelings of love and affection for one's spouses. Hence the very idea of contemplating polygamy, except for the greater benefit of the society could run shivers in a sincere Muslim's spine since Islam demands perfect balance between all one's wives in a polygamous household while human nature makes it impossible for a person to maintain such perfection but the Quran admonishes:

'incline not wholly to one so that you leave the other like a thing suspended.'[106]

These injunctions of the Quran in relation to the manner in which polygamy should be regulated in an Islamic household have been further supplemented with grave warnings by the Prophet of Islam[sa] who stated:

'If a man has two wives and he is inclined to one of them while neglecting the other, he shall be

---

[104] Ibid 4.4
[105] Ibid 4.130
[106] Ibid

**raised on the Day of Judgement with one of his
sides having been severed.'[107]**

Although Prophet Muhammad[sa] himself treated his wife with
equality in all matters over which he had control yet he often
supplicated:

**'My Lord! these are my dealing in matters over
which man has no control; so blame me not for
that which is in Thy power and not mine.'[108]**

The entire question of polygamy is therefore approached by
Islam in a very cautious manner and rather than encourage
it, Islam is the first religion which restricted its scope as
admitted by western scholars who state that the institution of
polygamy:

**'was fully accepted and legally recognised not
only among Arabs but also among other people
of that region. As a matter of fact, the Islamic
law, which seems today to have been full of
concessions on this subject, actually established
for the followers of Muhammad, certain
limitations upon polygamy which was in
practice without any limitations.'[109]**

Polygamy was and is to this day practised without limitation
in every non Islamic religion and culture and the failure of
these civilizations to regulate it in a proper manner has
resulted in an excessive abuse of an otherwise honourable
institution. In Judaism for instance, polygamy was excessively
practised and deplorably abused and while Christian
expositors of law denied the realities of life and forced their
congregation to the opposite extreme, the signs of

---

[107] Sunan Abu Daud
[108] Ibid
[109] Vaglieri, Laura Veccia. An Interpretation of Islam

unregulated polygamy are blatantly noticeable in their society as for instance evident from the following admission of a western scholar:

> **'Man lives in a state of polygamy in the civilized countries in spite of monogamy enforced by law. Out of hundred thousand men there would barely be one who could swear upon his death bed that he had never known but one single woman during his whole lifetime.'**[110]

Others westerners have condemned their society for 'wanton and brutal hypocrisy in being offended by legitimate polygamist solutions to its problems yet showing no indignation at its present state of monogamy with prostitution'[111] which is in truth unregulated polygamy without responsibility - polygamy being the state or practice of having more than one female mate. Yet another western scholar refers to this unregulated polygamy without responsibility in the west to state:

> **'In no part of the world is polygamy so prevalent as in Christiandom and in no part of the world is it so easy for a man to escape his obligations incurred by it. We imagine that if we refuse to recognise the fact of polygamy, we may refuse to recognise any obligations incurred by it. By enabling man to escape so easily from the obligations of his polygamous relationship, we encourage him if he is unscrupulous, to enter into them and place a premium on the immorality we loftily condemn. Our polygamy has no legal existence. The ostrich, it was once imagined, hides its head in the sand and**

---

[110] Nordan, Max. Conventional Lies of Our Civilization
[111] Ludokici, Anthony M. Woman. A Vindication

attempts to annihilate facts by refusing to look at them but there is only one known animal which adopts this course of action and it is called man.'[112]

Islam restricted the number of wives permissible in a polygamous structure of marriage and also laid down stringent conditions for regulating it in a proper manner. It offered a compromise to the either of the two extremes in so much that while forbidding excessive indulgence as found permissible in Judaism, it offered a practical solution to the problems faced by the Christian world on account of its refusal to accept the merits of polygamy. Hence it brought such civility and honour to the institutions of marriage and polygamy that non-Muslims scholars found themselves obliged to state:

'We must offer our deepest admiration to a religion which does not stop with a theory suited to the aspirations of the human race nor with establishing a code of the highest rules which man can live by but which goes to inculcate a philosophy of life; which puts basic principles of morality on a systematic and positive basis; which translates the duty of man towards himself and others into precise rules which are capable of evolution and which are compatible with the highest intellectual development, and, to crown it all, which provides a sanction of these laws. Islam is such a religion.'[113]

---

[112] Ellis, Havelock. The Psychology of Sex
[113] Vaglieri, Laura Veccia. An Interpretation of Islam

CHAPTER EIGHT

RIGHTS OF A DIVORCED WOMAN

Although Hebrew scriptures admit permissibility of divorce yet while these give men a license to free themselves from their wives by merely presenting to them a Bill of Divorce[1] - Biblical law maintains an absolute silence on a woman's right to divorce her husband since she is considered his property and as such does not possess an authority to exercise her choice to divorce him.[2]

The exclusively Christian scriptures on the other hand clearly deny women in ruptured marriages a right to separate themselves from their husbands or seek divorce under all circumstances. Hence one reads in the epistles of St. Paul:

---

[1] Deuteronomy 24.1
[2] Aid to Bible Understanding, Watch Tower & Bible Tract Soc., p. 459

> **'If a woman shall put away her husband, and be married to another, she committeth adultery.'[3]**

The scope of this law which imposes such stringent restrictions upon Christian women in strained marriages is further extended by Paul's demand that if a woman leaves her husband then she remain unmarried for the rest of her husband's mortal life[4] and where she is put away by him she remain loyal to him despite being discarded. She is not permitted to marry another man and if she does then according to Christian law she is to be considered to have committed adultery:

> **'A woman which hath an husband is bound by the law to her husband so long as he liveth: but of the husband is dead, she is loosed from the law of her husband. So then if, while her husband liveth, she be married to another man, she shall be called an adulteress.'[5]**

ISLAM ON DIVORCE

In an Islamic social structure, divorce is considered to be a hateful and a detestable thing[6] and the noble Quran not only admonishes couples in strained marriages to seek reconciliation but it even places a time limit as to how long a husband and a wife may lawfully stay away from each other.[7] It also imposes a duty upon the society to intervene and endeavour to bring about harmony in a strained marriage and states:

---

[3] Mark 10.12
[4] Corinthians 7.10/11
[5] Romans 7.2/3
[6] Sunan Abu Daud
[7] Al Quran 2.227

'If you apprehend a breach between husband and wife, then appoint an arbiter from among his people and an arbiter from among her people. If they desire reconciliation, Allah will bring about accord between husband and wife.'[8]

It is however possible that disagreement in a marriage may have been permitted by the couple to reach a point of no return and although Islam detests divorce yet it does not permit its prejudice to tread upon the emotional welfare and happiness of its congregation. In extreme situations where resort to separation cannot be avoided, it permits the inevitable and gives the couple a right to divorce but this permission may be resorted to only when it becomes extremely essential.[9] In such situations once again, Islam is seen to bestow equal rights upon the female species since the Quran states:

'wives have rights corresponding to those which the husbands have in an equitable manner.'[10]

Hence, a right to seek divorce is granted to women as much as it is granted to men an Islamic society. Therefore, a Muslim woman may, if she can establish that the failure of her marriage is beyond reconciliation seek freedom from her misery as much as a Muslim male who considers his marriage beyond repair although under circumstances where a wife sues for divorce, she may be required to return a part of what has been granted to her by her husband as dower and gifts during the course of the marriage. The Quran states in relation to such situations:

'It is not lawful for you to take anything of that which you have given your wives, unless the

---

[8] Ibid 4.36
[9] Sahih Bukhari 63.11
[10] Al Quran 2.229

> **husband and the wife should be afraid that they will not be able to observe the limits prescribed by Allah. In such cases there will be no sin on either of them in respect to that which the wife may give to get her freedom."**[11]

Muslim women may seek divorce from their husband on varied grounds and Islam does not place any unnecessary restrictions upon them. They are within their rights to demand divorce if they have been forced into giving consent of marriage[12] and they do not feel favourably inclined towards their husbands.[13] They may also file for divorce if they are unable to reconcile to their marriage[14] as well as on grounds of physical weakness or impotency of their spouse.[15] Women released from slavery may on being manumitted exercise their right to live with their husbands or else leave them[16] and in every one of these situations husbands are expected to respect the sentiments and wishes of their estranged brides or wives.[17] Nevertheless, this right is not expected to be exercised in a frivolous manner and Islam maintains that a spouse who seek separation without a legitimate cause shall be deprived of the fragrance of Paradise.[18] This right granted to Muslim women more than thirteen hundred years ago was unknown to the Judaeo-Christian countries until the present century when New Zealand granted its women a restricted right to seek divorce of their husbands in around 1912 while Australia followed suit in 1919 and in British law it became possible for the wife to divorce her husband in around 1923. Nonetheless, the present law in England and Wales permits

---

[11] Ibid 2.230
[12] Sahih Bukhari 62.43
[13] Ibid 63.3
[14] Ibid 63.12
[15] Ibid 63.7
[16] Ibid 63.14
[17] Sunan Ibn Majah
[18] Jami Tirmidhi

divorce on five grounds only none of which take into consideration personal sentiments of the couple.

TREATMENT OF WOMEN DURING PROCESS OF ISLAMIC DIVORCE

The process of divorce in Islam is a long and somewhat drawn out affair and involves pronouncement of divorce on three separate occasions extended over a waiting period of three courses - a period designed to give the couple sufficient opportunity to consider the implications of their action and possibly take remedial steps to bring about reconciliation. The Quran states in relation to this:

> 'Divorced women shall wait, concerning themselves, for a space of three courses. It is not lawful for them to conceal what Allah may have created in their wombs, if they believe in Allah and the Last Day. If their husbands should desire reconciliation during this period, they would have stronger right to the continuation of the marriage than that it should be dissolved. In such a case the wives have rights corresponding to those which the husbands have, in equitable reciprocity, though in certain situations men have been given an advantage above them."[19]

It should be observed here that the advantage which men have been given in this Quranic passage does not refer to the question of divorce. Islam demands that an estranged couple stay under one roof during this period of waiting before a divorce can be finalised and the Quran demands of men:

---

[19] Al Quran 2.229

'Lodge them during the prescribed period in the houses wherein you dwell, according to your means.'[20]

Hence, since an estranged couple are required to continue to live under one roof and share a common home wisdom demands that either one of the two partners be given the final authority in relation to the administration of the matrimonial home. In giving men a degree of advantage the Quran merely proposes to give the husbands the right to retain their authority which they commanded before the marriage became strained since they continue to be responsible for the maintenance of the household[21] and also of the estranged wife.[22] Nonetheless, the actual rights of a woman in relation to the question of divorce itself are not in any manner affected by this advantage given to men and while she continues to enjoy corresponding rights in equitable reciprocity if a husband institutes divorce proceedings against her, in situations where she decides to separate herself from the husband she commands an absolute right to determine her independent course of action.[23] Although according to Islamic conventions it is permissible to seek to influence a woman's decision within reason yet Islam insists that where she decides to seeks a divorce she may not be forced to change her decision against her own wishes.[24]

This prolonged stretch of time before a divorce can become absolute could impose an unbearable strain upon the emotional susceptibilities of the estranged couple - a strain further aggravated by the injunction that during this period the couple must live under the same roof. Therefore, the Quran proceeds to protect an estranged woman's rights with explicit injunctions to ensure that she is not mistreated nor

---

[20] Ibid 65.7
[21] Ibid 4.35
[22] Ibid 65.7
[23] Sahih Bukhari 63.12
[24] Ibid 63.16

are her rights denied. Hence, Islamic law requires that during this period of separation within the confines of a matrimonial home, husbands being stronger partners in a relationship conduct the affairs of their divorce in a considerate manner. It imposes a duty upon them not to only retain their estranged wives in their homes for the period of waiting and provide for their needs but also:

'harass them not to straiten them.'[25]

Islam does not permit husbands to either drive their wives out of their homes or expel them from their houses. The Quran demands of men:

'when you divorce your wives, observe the prescribed period for making the divorce effective, and reckon the period; and be mindful of your duty to Allah, your Lord. Turn them not out of their houses, nor should they leave their houses, unless they are guilty of manifest indecency.'[26]

Yet, while the law demands that husbands and wives remain under a common roof during this period and husbands are forbidden to force their wives into leaving their matrimonial home until the divorce has been made absolute, wives have been given a right to leave their matrimonial homes under exceptional circumstances. They may move to safer grounds if they fears their inability to maintain their composure or are afraid of their personal security. Women possess this right to make their own choice without any legal impediment or fear of recrimination[27] although Islamic convention insists that it

---

[25] Al Quran 65.7
[26] Ibid 65.2
[27] Sahih Bukhari 63.42

may only be exercised in exceptional cases and with extreme caution.[28]

ATTITUDE TOWARDS WOMEN ON COMPLETION OF PERIOD

During this entire period when a divorce proceeding is in progress, Islam repeatedly calls upon Muslims to seek reconciliation. The Quran alludes to compromise after the pronouncement of the first divorce[29] and if this opportunity is allowed to pass without reconciliation, it refers to it once again on the pronouncement of the second divorce.[30] After the prescribed period of waiting has expired but the third and final divorce has not been pronounced, the Quran calls upon reconciliation once again and states:

'When you divorce women and they approach the end of their appointed period, then either retain them in a becoming manner or send them away in a becoming manner.'[31]

If at this late point in time a basis of compromise is reached between the estranged couple and they decide to salvage their marriage then Islam admonishes guardians of women not to prevent them from remaining with their husbands[32] since according to the Quran, if they desire reconciliation then:

'their husbands have a stronger right to the continuation of marriage than that it should be irrevocably dissolved. And the wives have rights

---

[28] Ibid 63.41
[29] Al Quran 2.229
[30] Ibid 2.230
[31] Ibid 2.232
[32] Sahih Bukhari 63.44

corresponding to those which the husbands have, in equitable reciprocity.'[33]

However, if a compromise is not reached and divorce becomes inevitable then the Quran commands husbands to part with their divorced spouses in a decent and civilized manner and:

'send them away in a becoming manner.'[34]

To ensure that the rights of a wife being irrevocably divorced are not denied to her by the husband, the Quran enjoins that this final parting take place in the presence of witnesses. It states:

'send them away in a suitable manner and appoint two just persons from among you as witnesses; and bear true witness for the sake of Allah. This is an admonition for him who believes in Allah and the Last Day.'[35]

It is not permissible for men to cause any unnecessary hardship to women when they are leaving the homes of their former husbands nor are the husbands permitted to detain their divorced wives unlawfully or encroach upon their rights and therefore the Quran demands of men:

'retain them not wrongfully so that you may transgress against them. Whoso does that, surely wrongs his own soul.'[36]

---

[33] Al Quran 2.229
[34] Ibid 2.232
[35] Ibid 65.3
[36] Ibid 2.232

CONCERN OF PSYCHOLOGICAL WELFARE OF WOMEN

Islam is so thoroughly considerate of the physical and psychological welfare of women that it does not permit men to divorce their wives while they may be undergoing any kind of a physical and psychological phenomenon. Since women often suffer psychological depression during their monthly courses, the effects of this natural condition may bear heavily upon their physical and emotional beings. Hence, Islam does not permit divorce of women while they are undergoing the natural process of menstruation[37] and a divorce effected during this period is considered null and void.[38] The Quran lays down clear guidelines to ensure that wives are divorced during such periods only as is permissible in Islam and where it is difficult to determine the question of monthly courses it states:

'If you are in doubt as to the prescribed period for such of your women as have despaired of their monthly courses, then the prescribed period for them is three months, and also for those who have not had their monthly courses.'[39]

Expectant mothers are also saved emotional anguish of having to suffer the indignity and stress of an impending divorce during the crucial period of pregnancy when they not only require but also deserve the sympathy and understanding of their husbands. Therefore, Islam insists that expectant mothers cannot be divorced until they are delivered of their burden and the Quran states in relation to this:

---

[37] Sahih Bukhari 63.1
[38] Ibid 63.2
[39] Al Quran 65.5

'And for those who are with child, their period shall be until they are delivered.'[40]

These injunctions of the Quran which protect women from being divorced at such periods of their lives when they are either psychologically below par or in need of additional sympathy and loving care are charged with wisdom. The physical aspect of a marriage plays an important part in a couple's life but during periods of menstruation, Islam commands couples to abstain from intimate physical contact.[41] Therefore, in addition to the fact that women are psychologically at a very low peak when undergoing this natural process, the couple being denied an opportunity to intimacy may deprive them an occasion to discuss their matrimonial problems in an ideal environment. However, once women have completed this period, their psychological state undergoes a transformation and an added opportunity to restore normal physical relationship reverses the whole situation for the couple who are then in a much better position to consider their actions in a rational manner.

Similarly, where an estranged wife comes to expect a child while undergoing the threat of a divorce, the most hardened of hearts can be expected to soften at the expectation of the new arrival since children are a natural soothing factor in a strained marriage and the expected birth of a new child can go a long way in bringing about reconciliation in a strained marriage. One also needs to take into consideration that fact that a threat of divorce not only puts a heavy strain upon the couple but can also prove detrimental to the health of the mother and consequently the expected child. It would therefore be quite natural for the father of the expected offspring to review the entire situation if not for the sake of his wife then at least for the sake of his unborn child. On the

---

[40] Ibid
[41] Ibid 2.223

208

other hand, the mother, faced with the prospects of additional responsibility may have good cause to review her own situation since she could find the prospects of bringing up a child without the influence of a father or else the child's own father somewhat daunting. She could therefore seek to exert additional energy into bringing about a reconciliation in her strained marriage.

The additional time given to the couple under both these conditions can itself go a long way to heal the rift and return peace and tranquillity in their lives since time has after all been called the old common arbitrator and the greatest physician. This period of grace is in itself a great bounty bestowed upon women to protect them from the haste which is symbolic of a man's nature.[42]

FINANCIAL SECURITY

Islamic law on divorce also ensures that a divorced woman is not left in strained circumstances by her former husband. It demands a satisfactory financial arrangement for a divorcee and protects this right with an explicit injunction of the Quran:

'for the divorced woman also, there shall be provision according to what is fair. This is incumbent upon those who fear Allah.'[43]

The Quran admonishes husbands who divorce their wives not to repossess off these women what they have already given to them during the course of their marriage:

'It is not lawful for you to take away anything of that which you have given your wives.'[44]

---

[42] Ibid 21.38
[43] Ibid 2.242
[44] Ibid 2.230

The financial welfare of women whose marriages have not been consummated is also not disregarded in Islamic law and the Quran commands Muslim men to provide for their divorced wives in such cases also:

> 'it shall be no sin for you if you divorce women while you have not touched them, nor settled for them a dowry. But provide for them - the rich man according to his means and the poor man according to his means - a provision in a becoming manner. This is an obligation upon the virtuous. And if you divorce them before you have touched them, but have settled upon a dowry, then half of what you have settled shall be due from you, unless they remit, or he, in whose hand is the tie of marriage, should remit. And that what you remit is nearer to righteousness.'[45]

A wife divorced on mere suspicion of adultery by her husband retains the dowry or other material gifts bestowed upon her by her former spouse who according to Islamic law is not permitted to seek return of any material gift bestowed upon his former wife since Islam maintains that if his allegations against the divorced wife be false then he does not have a right to seek return of anything and if these unproven charges be true then he would still not have a right to seek the return of the dower because he has already consummated his marriage and received benefit of it.[46] A person who mistakenly marries a woman from the forbidden degree of consanguinity is not only obliged to divorce his wife but also permit her to leave without demanding the return of the dower.[47]

---

45 Ibid 2.237/238
46 Sahih Bukhari 63.32
47 Ibid 63.51

CARE OF DIVORCED MOTHERS

The Quran not only requires the husband of an expectant mother to provide for her needs until she is delivered of the child but it imposes a duty upon him to recompense her during the period she suckles his child which according to Islamic convention could take at least two years. The Quran demands of husbands who divorce their pregnant wives:

> 'If they be with child, spend on them until they are delivered of their burden. And if they give suck to the child for you, give them their due recompense, in consultation with one another according to what is customary; but if you meet with difficulty with each other, then let another suckle the child for the father. Let him who has abundance of means spend out of his abundance. And let him whose means of subsistence are straitened spend out of what Allah has given him.'[48]

A divorced mother retains an automatic custody of her children without having to seek judgement from a court of law and the father of the children is obliged to pay a maintenance allowance to her:

> 'mother shall give suck to their children for two whole years; for those who desire to complete the period of suckling. And a man to whom the child belongs shall be responsible for their maintenance and clothing according to usage. No soul is burdened beyond its capacity. Neither shall a mother be made to suffer on account of

---

[48] Al Quran 65.7/8

her child, nor shall he to whom the child belongs on account of the child.'[49]

A mother reserves the right of consent and consultation if her child needs to be weaned by a wet nurse and the husband is obliged by law to bear all the extra expense:

'If they both decide upon weaning the child by mutual consent and consultation, there is no blame on them. And if you desire to engage a wet nurse for your children, there shall be no blame on you, provided you pay what you have agreed in a fair manner. And fear Allah and know that Allah sees what you do.'[50]

Where a father of an infant child dies within its infancy, his heirs are under an obligation to assume the responsibility for the financial welfare of the mother and the child since the Quran states:

'and the same is incumbent upon the father's heirs.'[51]

A wife divorced on mere suspicion of adultery but not proven guilty of the offence retains her right to the custody of her children[52] and a child involved in a paternity dispute also remains in the custody of the mother.[53]

RIGHT TO RE MARRY

Islam not only permits divorced women to remarry but also admonishes former husbands and guardians of divorcees not

---

[49] Ibid 2.234
[50] Ibid
[51] Ibid
[52] Sahih Bukhari 63.35
[53] Ibid 60.211

to prevent them from engaging into matrimony as soon as the prescribed period of waiting in cases of divorce is over. The Quran states in relation to this:

'when you divorce women and they reach the end of their period, prevent them not from marrying their husbands if they agree between themselves in a decent manner.'[54]

Divorced women are free to consider their future course of action independently and their male guardians do not have a right to cause hindrance in what is decided by these women in relation to their own future[55] since Islamic thought maintains that they have a greater right to dispose themselves than their guardians.[56]

Hence one observes that unlike the Judaeo-Christian cultures which deny the female species a right to exercise their discretion in relation to their own lives and which impose a continued burden upon the female species to continue their lives with husbands who may have been imposed upon them by either their fathers in return for favours bestowed upon them by itinerant warriors whose support they sought[57] or else the Biblical law which throws them at the mercy of their assailants who physically abused them; forcefully defiled them; robbed them of their virginity; deprived them of their state of chastity and purity and also dented their honour and self-respect[58], Islam not only demands that women be consulted before they are given into marriage[59] but it also gives them a right to seek divorce if they have been coerced into giving consent by their guardians.[60]

---

[54] Al Quran 2.233
[55] Sahih Bukhari 63.44
[56] Sunan Abu Daud
[57] 1 Samuel 17.25 & 18.17
[58] Deuteronomy 22.28
[59] Sahih Bukhari
[60] Ibid

One also observes that while a Judaeo-Christian woman wrongfully accused of adultery by her jealous husband is made to return to him to conceive a seed of and for him[61], Islam permits women similarly accused to plead their innocence[62] and be freed of any matrimonial obligation to the husbands who accuse them of improper conduct in absence of witnesses.[63]

Biblical law also not only permits fathers to sell their daughters into slavery but the purchasers of these unfortunate women have the right to take them into their own harems or else be passed unto their male offspring and even Hebrew slaves. They are neither permitted to purchase their freedom[64] nor seek divorce by law and therefore they are at the total mercy of the men imposed upon them. Islam however not only permits slaves to purchase their own freedom[65] but manumitted and liberated female slaves are given the right to accept or reject the husbands imposed upon them during the period of their bondage by their masters.[66]

Hence these rights bestowed upon women to exercise their discretion in relation to their own lives are unique to Islam.

---

[61] Numbers 5.13/31
[62] Al Quran 4.7-10
[63] Sahih Bukhari
[64] Exodus 21.4/9
[65] Sahih Bukhari
[66] Sahih Bukhari

CHAPTER NINE

STATUS OF WIDOWS

Biblical law fails to make satisfactory provision for the financial welfare of Hebrew widows who could be left in dire circumstances particularly when their husbands die childless and they do not have any adult sons to depend upon. It's law of inheritance does not admit the right of widow to share the estate of their deceased husbands and therefore Hebrew widows are either required to return to their paternal homes[1] or else survive on the 'gleaner rights in the fields' which basically means that they live on left overs which the Hebrew farmers forget to harvest.[2] The only other security these unfortunate women have is the right to participate in the annual feast of Passover which lasts for a week where they

---

[1] Ruth 1.8
[2] Deuteronomy 24.19/21

may eat to their hearts content[3] or else 'come and eat and be satisfied' in the tithe once every three years.[4]

In the exclusively Christian congregation, widows fare relatively better than their Hebrew counterparts. Nevertheless, the burden of their welfare is initially thrust upon their kith and kin who may or may not, depending upon their own circumstances, be anxious to undertake the extra responsibility. Only those widows who are indeed destitute and do not have a close relation to depend upon become the responsibility of the Church but stringent rules in relation to the assistance of widows stipulate that the Church accept responsibility of only such widows as are over the age of sixty[5] and that too if these widows are:

> **'well reported of for good works; if she have brought up children, if she have lodged strangers, if she have washed the saints' feet, if she have relieved the afflicted, if she have diligently followed every good work.'[6]**

While elderly widows are assisted on the basis of their usefulness and obedience to the predominantly male hierarchy of the Church establishment, younger Christian women are denied assistance because of the risk factor that they may, after having drained the recourses of the Church, decide to engage into matrimony. Therefore, the New Testament demands that the Church fathers remain shy of assisting the younger widows and:

---

[3] ibid 16.10/14
[4] ibid 14.28/29
[5] 1 Tomothy 5.4/9
[6] ibid 5.11

> **'the younger widows refuse: for when they have begun to wax wanton against Christ, they will marry.'[7]**

Biblical laws also place an unnecessary restriction on the choice of a childless widow to marry a man outside the family of her own deceased husband and states that:

> **'If brethren dwell together, and one of them die, and have no child, the wife of the dead shall not marry unto a stranger: her husband's brother shall go in unto her; and take her to him to wife, and perform the duty of an husband unto her.'[8]**

Where a levirate marriage terminates in her being left childless again, she is obliged to wife yet another brother of her deceased husbands but if that is temporarily not possible on account of the age of her deceased husband's surviving brother, she is sent to her parents' home to await puberty of the child although her in-laws may have absolutely no intention to restore her to her former position as a daughter-in-law in the household of her deceased husband.[9] She has to therefore wait in anticipation and possibly be reduced to play the harlot in her father's house.[10]

If a widow chooses to remain behind and administer the property of her deceased husband and her in-laws permit her to do that[11], she stands the possibility of being purchased by a remote kinsman of her deceased husband who redeems his property. In this event, she too becomes the property of the kinsman.[12]

---

[7] ibid
[8] Deuteronomy 25.5
[9] Genesis 38.11
[10] ibid 38.14/24
[11] Ruth 1.8/18
[12] ibid 4.5/13

WIDOWS IN ISLAM

Islam does not reduce the widows in its society to such dire circumstances. It accepts total responsibility of these unfortunate victims of fate and also their offspring. The system of Zakat instituted as an essential pillar of Islamic faith in the opening years of Prophet Muhammad's[sa] ministry was devised to cope with the requirements of - amongst other, destitute widows and their households irrespective of their religious inclinations, conduct, piety or standing in a society. The Quran states that in every 'righteous person's wealth, there is a portion due to the needy who need help whether it is solicited or not'[13] and it requires Muslims to:

'render to thy kin their due and the needy and the wayfarer, and squander not thy substance extravagantly.'[14]

Quranic injunctions are extremely explicit that the poor in an Islamic society be provided with the essential needs to sustain their life, whether these be widows, orphans or prisoners of war and the Quran demands that this be done for pleasure of God and for return of gratitude from human beings. It states:

'feed the poor, the orphan and the captive for the love of Allah, assuring them: We feed you only for Allah's pleasure. We desire no return nor thanks from you.'[15]

A Muslim who concerns himself with the affairs of widows and assists them to the best of his ability has been placed in high regard by Islam. The Prophet of Islam, Hadhrat Muhammad[sa] declared:

---

[13] Al Quran 51.20
[14] ibid 17.27
[15] ibid 76.9/10

'One who manages the affairs of the widow is like one who exerts himself hard in the way of Allah or one who fasts in the day and stands up for prayer in the night..'[16]

FINANCIAL SECURITY OF WIDOWS

Widows in an Islamic society are not only granted financial security under the institution of Zakat, their welfare is not entirely subjected to generosity and charity as in the Judaeo-Christian cultures. The Quran grants them an automatic right to inherit from the estates of their deceased husbands and to ensure that they are neither deprived of their due nor exploited in the period of their grief, it lays down their share of inheritance by law and states:

'They shall have a fourth of that which you leave, if you have no child; but if you have a child, then they shall have an eighth of that which you leave, after the payment of any bequests made by you and your debts.'[17]

It also stipulates that husbands leave behind an additional share of their inheritance to their wives beside the generous provisions made for them under the Islamic Law of Inheritance - an amount which ought to last for at least the first year of their being widowed. It states:

'those of you who die and leave behind wives shall bequeath to their wives provision for a year.'[18]

---

[16] Sahih Bukhari 73.25 [26]
[17] Al Quran 4.13
[18] ibid 2.241

A Muslim widow is therefore much more secure in her grief than her counterpart in the Judaeo-Christian congregation. She is considered a person within her own right and she stands to inherit from her deceased husband irrespective of whether she has a male issue or not. She does not have to go through the humiliating experience of a levirate marriage against her consent to secure a right to her deceased husband's wealth nor can she be made to burden the financial resources of her parents where a levirate marriage is not possible.

A widow whose husband fails to make a satisfactory provision for her and is left financially insecure and destitute has her right to assistance secured by the injunctions of the Quran. The state and the society is under divine obligation to assume responsibility of her welfare whether she is past marriageable age or a younger widow who may yet decide to marry. She is neither dependent on the left overs in the Judaic culture nor on the selective system of the Christian congregation.

RIGHT TO RE MARRY

A Muslim widow also reserves the right to re marry after the prescribed period of waiting and Islam on the death of her husband. The Quran encourages marriage of widows and requires parents or guardians to:

> 'arrange marriages for widows from among you."[19]

Islam gives widowed women an independent right to decide upon their future course of action and does not place any unnecessary restriction upon their choice. The Quran states:

---

[19] Al Quran 24.33

'as for those of you who die and leave behind wives, these shall wait concerning themselves for four months and ten days. And when they have reached the end of this period, no blame shall attach to you concerning anything that they do with regard to themselves in a decent manner.'[20]

It admonishes Muslim men to respect the grief of widows and not take advantage of their situation while it encourages them to marry these unfortunate victims of fate and provide them with homes after the prescribed period of waiting for these widows is over. It states:

'There shall be no blame on you in hinting at a proposal of marriage to these women or in contemplating the possibility in your minds. Allah knows that you will think of them in that connection; but do not enter into any secret arrangement with them, beyond conveying some indication to them of your inclination. And resolve not on the marriage until after the expiry of the period of waiting. Be sure Allah knows what is in your mind, so be mindful of Him.'[21]

---

[20] ibid 2.235
[21] ibid 2.236

CHAPTER ELEVEN

ORPHANS AND THEIR RIGHTS

Orphans in a Biblical society fare no better than widows in the Judaeo-Christian congregation except that they too are given gleaner rights which effectively means that they are permitted to go to the fields and orchards and also vineyards to gather all that the owners of these lands have forgotten to harvest. For instance, Biblical law states in relation to the right of the orphans:

> 'When thou cuttest down thine harvest in thy
> field, and hast forgot a sheaf in the field, thou
> shalt not go again to fetch it: it shall be for the
> stranger, for the fatherless, and for the widow.
> When thou beatest thine olive tree, thou shalt
> not go over the boughs again: it shall be for the
> stranger, the fatherless, and for the widow.
> When thou gatherest the grapes of thy vineyard,
> thou shalt not glean it afterwards: it shall be for

> the stranger, for the fatherless, and for the
> widow."[1]

Beside these leftovers to which orphans of the Judaeo-Christian society are entitled every year, Biblical law gives them a right to attend the annual Festival of Gathering and feed themselves to their full.[2] Or else once in every three years, they are entitled to the 'tithe of the increase of harvest' - that is, only ten percent of the increase of the harvest which is left outside the gates of their cities by Hebrew landowners.[3]

In addition to this lack of enthusiasm towards the welfare of orphans in the Biblical scriptures, female orphans suffer a further handicap when the law denies them the right to inherit from their estates of their fathers except in the most exceptional circumstances where there are no male offspring to inherit.[4] Orphaned children do not fare any better in Christian scriptures. The New Testament gives mere lip service to the rights care of orphans[5] and fails to make any specific provision to either safeguard their rights or else promote their welfare. Nor does it grant any particular right to these unfortunate victims of fate deprived of a right to inherit from the estates of their fathers.

ISLAM ON ORPHANS

Islam on the other hand makes excellent provisions, not only for the male but also female orphans in its society. The Quran grants female offspring a right to inherit from the estate of her parents to state:

---

[1] Deuteronomy 24.19/21
[2] ibid. 16.10/11
[3] ibid. 14.28/29
[4] Numbers 27.8
[5] James 1.27

> **'For men, as well as women, there is a share in
> that which their parents and near relatives
> leave, whether it be little or much, a share which
> has been determined.'[6]**

It then proceeds to safeguard the share of the female offspring to ensure that they are not deprived of their rightful portion whether there are male children to inherit or not. It states:

> **'Allah commands you concerning your children
> as follows: the share of a male is as much as a
> share of two females: but if there are only
> females, two or more, then they shall have two
> thirds of what the deceased should leave and if
> there is only one, then only one she shall have a
> half.'[7]**

These provisions made for a female orphan to inherit from the estate of her parents within her own right and her mother's independent right to share the wealth of her deceased husband[8] ensures that an orphan is not left in dire financial circumstances. Yet, in addition to this extremely generous provision made for the orphan and her mother, Islam enjoins husbands to leave an additional provision for their widows which should last them for a period of at least one year. The Quran states:

> **'Those of you who die leaving them surviving
> widows shall bequeth to their widows provision
> for a year.'[9]**

---

[6] Al Quran 4.8
[7] ibid. 4.12
[8] ibid. 4.13
[9] ibid. 2.241

An orphaned child is therefore left in relative financial security by the Quranic injunctions which provide her and her widowed mother with ample resources to sustain life and not be dependent upon the generosity and charity of other people particularly when her father dies leaving behind him a reasonable amount of wealth.

Islam extends this financial security to a child who becomes an orphan even after her mother has been divorced. Her right to inherit from her father's estate is not diminished if her mother is divorced by her physical father and in the event of her becoming an orphan after the divorce of her parents, she not only stands to inherit her share from the property of her father but Islamic law imposes a duty of the child's welfare as well as that the mother upon the heirs of the child's father:

> **'In cases of divorce, mothers shall give suck to their children for two whole years, where it is desired to complete the suckling, and the father of the child shall be responsible for the maintanance of the mother during that period, according to usage. No one shall be burdened beyond his capacity. No mother shall be made to suffer on account of her child, and no father shall be made to suffer on account of his child, and the same is the obligation of the heirs.'[10]**

Islam also requires relatives of orphans to concern themselves with the welfare of their kinsfolk and give them a part of the division of their wealth without causing any distinction between male and female species. The Quran states in relation to this:

> **'At the time of the division of the inheritance, if there are present other relations and orphans**

---

[10] ibid. 2.234

**and the needy, give them also something out of
it and speak to them graciously.'**[11]

It also demands that Muslims assist their relatives in their hour of need as a right due to them.[12] In addition to this, Islam has instituted the system of Zakat for the welfare needy and has made it obligatory upon every Muslim to contribute to the welfare of the needy whether assistance is sought by them or not.[13] It considers feeding orphans an act of righteousness through which man can achieve unlimited spiritual progress and the Quran states in relation to orphans in particular, whether male or female:

**'They ask thee concerning the orphans. Say,
'Promotion of their welfare is an act of great
goodness and if you mix with them, they are
your brethren. Allah knows him who seeks to
make mischief from him who seeks to promote
the welfare of the orphans."**[14]

PROTECTION OF PROPERTY

The injunctions of the Quran takes particular care to protect the property of orphans and requires of Muslims to administer their assets in a proper manner until they acquire maturity. It states:

**'Approach not the property of the orphans,
except in a manner which is best till they attain
maturity."**[15]

---

[11] ibid. 4.9

[12] ibid. 90.11/17
[13] ibid. 51.20
[14] ibid. 2.221
[15] ibid. 6.153

Islam demands that Muslims fulfill their obligations in relation to the property of the orphans in a becoming manner lest they be questioned about it[16] and while it gives executors the right to benefit from the administration of the estate left behind to the orphans, it not only puts stringent conditions on them to ensure that their permitted expenditure is not extravagant but also forbids people of means and sustenance to benefit from the services rendered towards the administration of the estate of orphans.[17] The Quran also admonishes Muslims not to have any covert design or intent in relation to the property of the orphan:

> 'Give to the orphans their property and
> exchange not the bad for good, and devour not
> their property by mixing it with your own.
> Surely, it is a great sin.'[18]

Islamic scriptures views the embezzlement of an orphan's property very seriously and the Quran promises severe chastisement for those who disregard the rights of orphans. It states:

> 'Surely, those who devour the property of
> orphans unjustly, only swallow fire into their
> bellies and shall enter a blazing fire.'[19]

The Prophet of Islam, Hadhrat Muhammad[sa] was himself extremely concerned with the welfare of the orphans - particularly the female orphans in an Islamic society. He declared that:

> 'One who manages the affairs of the widow and
> the needy is like one who exerts himself hard in

---

[16] ibid. 17.35.
[17] ibid. 4.7
[18] ibid. 4.3
[19] ibid. 4.11

the way of Allah or one who stands up for prayer in the night and fasts in the day.'[20]

Traditions also indicate that the Prophet of Islam[sa] held guardians of orphans in a very high regard. He is stated to have put his index and middle fingers together and declared:

'I and the person who looks after an orphan and provides for one will be like this.'[21]

MARRIAGE WITH ORPHANS

The Quran lays a particular stress upon the marriage of the orphan girls and requires Muslims to seek brides from amongst the orphans under their care but it demands that Muslims who seek to marry them ought to deal equitably with them and if they fear that they shall not be able to deal in an equitable manner, then they ought to marry other women as appear agreeable to them.[22] The purpose of this commandment is to ensure that the rights of female orphans, particularly their wealth is not devoured by their ward who may seek to marry them and therefore hope to gain a right over their wealth through matrimony. This is indicated by the Quranic verse:

'They seek directions from thee in the matter of marrying more women than one. Say to them: Allah has given you directions concerning them. The commandment given to you elsewhere in the Book has reference to orphan girls whom you give not what is prescribed for them and yet whom you desire to marry, and to unprotected

---

[20] Sahih Bukhari
[21] ibid. 73.24
[22] Al Quran 4.3/4

**female children. You have also been
commanded to deal equitably with orphans.'[23]**

Islam has showed such concern for the rights of female orphans that Muslims are forbidden from marrying orphan girls in their care unless they were given an appropriate dowry[24] which might be given to them by another suitor.[25] Islam is therefore extremely insistent that the right of orphans in every sphere of their life be protected and Prophet Muhammad[sa] declared that their rights should be protected as an article of Islamic faith. He stated:

**'I declare it sinful any failure to safeguard the
rights of two weak one, the orphans and
women.'[26]**

---

[23] 23. ibid. 4.128
[24] Sahih Bukhari 44.7
[25] ibid. 51.22
[26] Sunan al Nasai

CHAPTER ELEVEN

FEMALE SLAVES AND PRISONERS OF WAR

Female slaves have probably been the most unfortunate human beings known to the history of mankind since in every civilization they have had to suffer such physical torture and emotional humiliation as does not befit human dignity. They were reduced to a state of servitude to toil endlessly under compulsion by their masters who also had a legal right to buy and sell them as commodity. Besides being labourers in the household of their owners, female slave served as objects of sexual gratification to their masters and other male members of his household. They could be prevailed upon her to serve the physical needs of a master's friends and guests or else be forced into a life of prostitution for monetary gain by their owners. They were also denied a right to marry although they could contract informal marriage arrangements which had no legal validity and children born of such unions were considered illegitimate for the purpose of the law.

Biblical law itself permits acquisition of male and female slaves from amongst the pagan people as well the Hebrew nation[1] and it also recognises a father's right to sell himself or his children into slavery[2] to either take care of his debt or else relieve poverty in his household[3] but whereas a male slave cannot be compelled to serve his purchaser as a bond servant[4] and is also permitted to redeem himself and his wife and children if he entered the service of his master with them[5], a female sold into slavery by her father may expect to remain a slave for the rest of her mortal life since Biblical law denies her the right to either redeem herself or purchase her freedom. It states:

> **'And if a man sell his daughter to be a maid servant, she shall not go out as the male servants do.'[6]**

A female slave can also expect herself to be taken into the harem of her purchaser or be presented to his sons.[7] Biblical law also gives her purchaser a right to consign her to a male slave to wife in which event the children born of this arrangement become the property of her owner and whereas her male Hebrew partner is permitted to redeem himself or purchase his freedom, she and her litter remain the property of her owner:

> **'Now these are the judgements which thou shalt set before them. If thou buy a Hebrew servant, six years he shall serve; and in the seventh he shall go out free for nothing. If he came in by himself, he shall go out by himself: if he were**

---

[1] Leviticus 25.44
[2] ibid. 25.40/42
[3] Nehemiah 5.5
[4] Leviticus 25.39
[5] Exodus 21.2/3
[6] ibid. 21.7
[7] ibid. 21.8/9

married, then his wife shall go out with him. If his master have given him a wife, and she have born him sons or daughters; the wife and her children shall be her master's, and he shall go out by himself.'[8]

Women prisoners taken into captivity are also treated rather harshly by Biblical law which condemns all female captives as are not virgins to death and reduces others to slavery. Biblical ordinances in relation to these prisoners of war states:

'Now therefore kill every male among the little ones, and kill every woman that hath known man by lying with him. But all the women children, that have not known a man by lying with him, keep alive for yourself.'[9]

A beautiful woman captive may be forced into marriage to her captor if her beauty captivates him and he has a desire for her whether she wants to be joined into matrimony or not with a person who may have been responsible for the death of her parents and family. Biblical law also subjects her to severe humiliation before her captor is lawfully permitted to take her unto himself as a wife. It states:

'When thou goest forth to war against thine emenies, and the Lord thy God hath delivered them into thine hands, and thou hast taken them captive, and seest among the captives a beautiful woman, and hast a desire unto her, that thou wouldst have her to thy wife, then thou shall bring her home to thine house; and she shall shave her head, and pare her nails; and she shall put the raiment of her captivity from

---

[8] ibid. 21.1/4
[9] Numbers 31.17/18

> **off her; and shall remain in thine house, and bewail her father and mother a full month: after that thou shalt go in unto her, and be her husband, and she shall be thy wife."[10]**

ISLAM ON HUMAN CAPTIVES

Islam is the first religion which gave these slaves as well as prisoners of war a hope in life. In the first instance, the Quran effectually abolished the practice of taking human beings as captives except during the course of a major battle and stated:

> **'It behoves not a Prophet to take captives, except in the course of regular fighting. To take captives in the course of skirmishes and small scale action would mean that you are merely seeking temporal gain, whereas Allah desires for you the Hereafter."[11]**

Nonetheless, this permission is not a licence for Muslims to take human captives during the course of a major war and reduce them to slavery. The Quran demands that prisoners of war be kept captives only for as long as a state of emergency exists after which they are to be either released as an act of grace or be ransomed:

> **'When you meet in battle those who have disbelieved, smite their necks; and after the slaughter fasten tight the bonds, until the war lays aside its burden. Then either release them as**

---

[10] Deuteronomy 21.10/13
[11] Al Quran 8.68

233

a favour, or in return for ransom. That is the ordinance."[12]

Islam maintains that to spend one's wealth to ransom slaves is an act of righteousness[13] and a means to acquire unlimited spiritual progress.[14] Yet, while it encouraged Muslims to manumit slaves and declared that their charitable act would shield them against the chastisement of hell[15], it also remained cautious of the risks which could be encountered with a sudden implementation of its policy to release the slaves from bondage. Therefore, to spare the slaves a traumatic and possible a fatal experience, Islam phased out slavery gradually and consequently imposed a continued burden upon Muslims to provide for the needs of their slaves in a similar manner in which they provided for their own needs.[16] Nevertheless, this did not diminish a slave's right to seek freedom[17] nor did it restrict one to seek assistance in securing freedom from bondage[18] since Islam gave them an absolute right to purchase their own freedom.[19]

TREATMENT OF SLAVES

Since wisdom demanded that slavery be phased out gradually to assist the slaves to assimilate in the society, Islam endeavoured to break the taboos attached to slavery by giving them recognition and improving their lot. The Prophet of Islam[sa] admonished Muslims that slaves were their fellow

---

[12] ibid. 47.5
[13] ibid. 2.178
[14] ibid. 90.11/14
[15] Sahih Bukhari 46.1
[16] Sahih Muslim
[17] Sahih Bukhari 46.23
[18] ibid. 46.24
[19] ibid. 8.70

human being and entitled to be treated with respect and equity. He stated:

> **'Your slaves are your brethren upon whom Allah has given you authority. So, if one has one's brethren under one's control, one should feed them with the like of what one eats and clothe them with the like of what one wears. You should not overburden them with what they cannot bear, and if you do so, then help them in their task.'**[20]

Traditions also insisted upon treating the slaves kindly and educating them so that they could gain confidence in themselves and also become socially acceptable in a society.[21]

MARRIAGE OF SLAVES

To provide a favourable environment for the assimilation of the freed slaves in the society, the Quran exhorted Muslims to arrange marriages for the slaves in their possession and stated:

> **'Arrange marriages for the widows from among you, and for your males and female slaves who are fit for marriage. If they be poor, Allah will grant them means out of His bounty.'**[22]

The purpose of this injunction was to provide the slaves with relative material security and also save them the traumatic experience of having to survive in a competitive society in which they formerly existed as slaves only. The Quran also encouraged owners to marry female slaves in their possession

---

[20] ibid. 73.44
[21] ibid. 46.14
[22] Al Quran 24.33

as an act of righteousness[23] and therefore bestow dignity and honour upon them in an environment already known to them.

Islam also laid a particularly heavy stress upon the need to treat female slaves in a decent manner and to educate them so that they become socially acceptable and are able to function effectively as individual human beings in a society which traditionally looked upon them with scorn and contempt. It also exhorted Muslims not to be discouraged by the stigma attached to slavery and encouraged them to free female slaves in their possession and marry them. It declared that:

> **'He who has a slave girl and educates her and treats her nicely and then manumits and marries her shall get a double reward.'[24]**

The beauty of these ordinances is illustrated by the fact that a female slave is, in the first instance taught good manners and given enough education to be able to determine on the question of her own welfare. She is then granted absolute freedom to make a free choice and if she decides not to marry her former master, she is within her right to refuse since Islam denies men a right to inherit women against their will and the Quran demands:

> **'O ye who believe, it is not lawful for you to inherit women against their will.'[25]**

A female slave is therefore sufficiently protected by Islamic law to be a guardian of her own physical being and sufficiently liberated to have a right to free choice in matters of matrimony. She cannot be forced into marriage against her since Traditions demand that a woman shall not be married

---

[23] ibid. 4.4
[24] Sahih Bukhari 46.14
[25] Al Quran 4.20

until she has been consulted and her consent obtained.[26] Islam extended the scope of this ordinance further to include female slaves also:

> **'a lady slave shall not be married until she is consulted, and the virgin shall not given in marriage until her permission is granted.'[27]**

Since Islam had already established a woman's right to seek divorce[28] and marriages solemnised with a coerced consent of a woman are subject to annulment[29] - a liberated female slave is therefore permitted to exercise her right to freedom from a bond of matrimony imposed upon her during her days of bondage[30] and she cannot be forced to accept the husband of her captivity against her will if she chooses not to spend the rest of her life with him.[31]

Islam also demanded that female slaves or prisoners of war married by Muslims be given their dower[32]. It also bestowed the status of free persons to female slaves who migrated to find security amongst Muslims and granted them same rights as other emigrants. It also imposed an additional burden over Muslims to pay her price to the pagans if a treaty existed between them but under no circumstances return then to their pagan masters.[33]

---

[26]   Sahih Bukhari 67.42
[27]   ibid. 86.11
[28]   ibid. 63.12
[29]   ibid. 62.43
[30]   ibid. 63.15
[31]   ibid. 63.16
[32]   ibid. 62.14
[33]   ibid. 63.19

SECURITY AGAINST SEXUAL ABUSE

The dignity which Islam bestowed upon the female slaves may be illustrated by such other Quranic injunctions as require Muslims to take particular care of emotional sensitivities of these unfortunate women. For instance, Muslims are were required to respects the wishes of the female slaves and not to disregard their desire to remain chaste in their lives. The Quran admonished:

> 'Compel not your slave girls into unchaste life
> when they desire to remain chaste in order to
> seek the frail goods of this life. And whoever
> compels them, then surely after their
> compulsion, Allah will be Forgiving and Merciful
> to them.'[34]

Muslims are also discouraged from taking advantage of women taken as captives during the course of a battle. They are admonished not to indulge in casual sex with female captives of war[35] nor force them into any kind of an illegal sexual activity for personal physical satisfaction[36] or monetary gain.[37] A person who transgress the limits to engage in sexual activity with female slave is liable to severe punished under the Islamic penal code even if such activity was engaged in ignorance of the law.[38]

---

[34] Al Quran 24.34
[35] Sahih Bukhari 62.97
[36] ibid. 34.111
[37] ibid. 63.51
[38] ibid. 37.4

EVIDENCE OF FEMALE SLAVES

Islam elated the status of the female slaves in its society to an extent that it conferred upon them the right to bear evidence, including in cases of slander involving the most honoured and noble Muslims. It has also given credibility to the testimony of female slaves and held their evidence in high regard.[39] The testimony of insignificant female slaves has also been found admissible in matrimonial cases and Muslim couples commanded to go through the agony of a painful divorced.[40]

It is a recorded fact of history that no other religion or culture gave such exceptional rights to female slaves and prisoners of war as was bestowed upon them by Islam - a religion which not only safeguarded their rights but also sufficiently raised their spirits to consider themselves as human beings no lesser than their masters and mistresses. Their being slaves was merely an unfortunate reality of circumstances but Islam gave them a realisation that they were human beings - protected and respected as individuals. The Quran declares believing female slaves to be better than idolatrous women[41] and even considers them spiritually fit to lead Muslim nobility in prayers.[42]

---

[39] ibid. 48.2
[40] ibid. 48.13
[41] Al Quran 2.222
[42] Sahih Bukhari 11.54

CHAPTER TWELVE

THE PRECEPT OF PURDAH

The Islamic purdah has often been held synonymous to the eastern custom of keeping women in seclusion with clothing that conceal them completely and it has not only been suggested that its purpose has been impose a form of sexual apartheid in which women are never permitted to be seen by men who are not members of the immediate family but that its aim is to keep women in their place[1] - possibly implying that its objective is to keep women in subjection to their male counterparts. However, such opinions in relation to the precept of purdah in Islam are based upon the observed customs in the eastern cultures rather than the requirements of the Islamic law.

Islam as a religion proposes to deliver humanity from the depths of social and moral profligacy to which it has sunk throughout its history and therefore to achieve its purpose it

---

[1]

has, from the beginning, aspired to create a permanent infrastructure of an excellent society in which it is possible for man to live a decent and a moral life. Since it concerns itself with the physical, moral and spiritual welfare of mankind, it has devised certain rules of human conduct which are essential in mankind's endeavour to discard evil - the requirement of purdah being only one of them - and therefore to view the Islamic precept of purdah as a custom which imposes an unnecessary burden upon women or which them in seclusion is to look at it from a very narrow point of view and display sheer ignorance of the entire concept since purdah in Islam embraces a much wider meaning than a mere mode of dress or else how a female should regulate her movements.

When looked at in its proper perspective and from a broader spectrum, the Quranic injunctions relating to purdah are neither directed towards women alone nor do these impose a code of conduct and behaviour upon the female species only. In fact, these embrace every aspect of human activity, physical as well as psychological and the purpose of these regulations is to restrain, arrest and finally eradicate every animalistic passion inherent in a human being's nature - a nature which according to Islam is not free from weakness and a nature which is wont to incites and command evil[2] even though God Almighty has fashioned mankind in the best of moulds[3] and has endowed it with perfect faculties to achieve an infinite moral and spiritual progress.[4]

---

[2] Al Quran 12.54
[3] ibid. 95.5
[4] ibid. 32.10

ISLAM AND CHASTITY

Islam demands an extremely high standard of morality its society and forbids every kind of indecency, evil and transgression.[5] Chastity, which in a simple language means the state of being sexually pure and chaste involves abstinence from any kind of unlawful sexual activity and Islam defines this state of physical purity as an essential pre requisite to achieving any kind of an evil free society. It places chastity extremely high on its list of values and moral virtues and abhors every form of lewdness. The Quran depicts adultery as an abominable sin - as grave as the sin of associating partners with God Almighty or deliberate murder and promises severe chastisement to those who indulge in it.[6] Traditions consider adultery to be one of the three greatest sins which ought to be avoided[7] and the Prophet of Islam[sa] depicted adultery as a sin, as grave as associating partners with God or committing infanticide.[8] The Quran has repeatedly drawn the attention of mankind towards this abominable sin and admonished Muslims to abstain from this evil. It states:

'Do not even approach adultery; surely it is a foul thing and an evil way.'[9]

Islamic ideology maintains that the life of faith is taken away from a person who commits illegal sexual intercourse[10] and therefore adultery has been viewed with such contempt and revulsion that Prophet Muhammad[sa] was advised by God not to admit anyone into the fold of Islam unless one promised

---

[5] ibid. 16.91
[6] ibid. 25.69/70
[7] Sahih Bukhari 82.6
[8] ibid. 60.222
[9] Al Quran 17.33
[10] Sahih Bukhari 81.2

to refrain from this sin[11] and the Quran forbade Muslims to have any kind of an association with an adulterer or an adulteress.[12] But a system which proposes to set a desired standard of morality in its society is also required to define certain rules of conduct through which the desired end may be achieved. But, to merely promulgate rules and issue decrees without actually striving to provide a favourable environment for the practical implementation of these would be to hawk at eagles with a dove. Therefore, Islam not only defines rules which enables Muslims to achieve the desired standard of morality in their society but also proposes to create an environment in which these rules can be practically implemented - and for this, Islam is neither embarassed nor does it need apologise.

The existence of evil in a society has always been an issue of major concern to nearly every civilization and every society has aspired to find a magic formula which would eventually rid mankind of its very existence. Islam addresses itself to this issue also but since it is appreciative of the weakness and complexity of human nature is weak, Traditions admit that:

'Allah has written for the children of Adam their share of adultery which they commit inevitably. The adultery of the eye is the sight to gaze at forbidden things, the adultery of the tongue is the talk and the inner wishes and desires and the private parts testify or deny all this.'[13]

Yet, Islam does not adopt a fatalistic attitude and endeavours to devise such rules of conduct as may lessen the hazard suffered by mankind. This concept has been beautifully explained by one the greatest exponents of Islamic thought the world has ever known who discussed the means which

---

[11] Al Quran 60.13
[12] ibid. 24.4
[13] Sahih Bukhari 74.12

God Almighty has appointed for discarding evil and stated that in Islam:

'The moral qualities which the true Creator has appointed for the discarding of evil are known by four names in Arabic which has a specific name for all human concepts, behaviours and morals. The first of these morals is called Itham, that is to say, chastity. This expression connotes the virtue that is related to the faculty of procreation of men and women. Those men and women would be called chaste who refrain altogether from illicit sex and all approaches to it, the consequences of which is disgrace and humiliation for both parties in the world, and chastisement in the hereafter, and dishonour and grave harm for those related to them. '

'As this vice and its preliminaries can be practiced by both men and women, the Holy Book of God sets forth directions for both men and women in this context. It says:

"Say to the believing men that they lower their gaze and guard their modesty. That is purer for them. And say to the believing women that they restrain their looks and guard their modesty, and that they display not their beauty except that which is apparent thereof, and that they draw their head covering over their bosom. And that they strike not their feet so that what they hide of their ornaments may become known. And turn you to Allah altogether, O believers, that you may succeed." [Al Nur 31/32]'[14]

---

[14] Ahmad, [Hadhrat] Mirza Ghulam. The Philosophy of the

These directions laid down by the injunctions of the Quran, when read in a proper context indicate that the Prophet Muhammad[sa] was required by God Almighty to:

> "Direct the believing men to restrain their eyes from looking at women outside the prohibited degrees so openly as to be sexually exicted by them, and to cultivate the habit of guarding their own looks. They should safeguard all their senses. For instance, they should not listen to the singing or beguiling voices of women outside the prohibited degrees nor should they listen to descriptions of their beauty. This is a good way of preserving the purity of their looks and hearts. In the same way direct the believing women that they should safeguard their eyes from looking at men outside the prohibited degrees and should safegaurd their ears against listening to the passionate voices of such men. They should cover up their beauty and should not disclose it to anyone outside the prohibited degrees. They should draw their head coverings across their bosom and should cover up their heads and ears and temples. They should not strike their feet on the ground like dancers. These are directions which can safeguard against moral stumbling."[15]

A thorough analysis of the Quranic injunctions which relate to the observance of purdah should therefore, in the first instance indicate that that Islam does not impose the rules of safeguarding chastity upon women only but that these rules

---

Teachings of Islam, pp. 21/22
[15] ibid. 22.23

are imposed upon both sexes - male[16] as much as female[17] and to allege that the Quran inflicts unnecessary restrictions upon its womenfolk in this relation is either a biased view based upon thorough ignorance of Islamic teachings or else sheer prejudice against it.

MODESTY TO BE OBSERVED THROUGH COVERING NAKEDNESS

The wisdom of wearing a dress which does not expose a human body unnecessarily has not only been recognised in most cultured civilizations of the world but has been found essential by mankind from the beginning of time. Biblical scriptures maintain that no sooner did God create a man and a woman that He proceeded to cover their nakedness which Adam and Eve happened to lose after their temptation by the devil and their subsequent fall from grace. Nonetheless, the couple were not content to continue in their natural state so when:

'the eyes of them both were opened, and they knew they were naked; and they sewed fig leaves together, and made themselves aprons.'[18]

The Bible then states that although Adam and Eve had already covered their nakedness with aprons made out of fig leaves - at some later stage Hod Himself proceeded to make some clothing for the couple:

'Unto Adam also, and to his wife, did the Lord God make coats of skins, and clothed them.'[19]

---

[16] Al Quran 24.31
[17] ibid. 24.32
[18] Genesis 3.7
[19] ibid. 3.21

Mankind has therefore covered its nakedness with clothing since the beginning of time but as the world became more complex, every society set its own minimum standards with greater stress being put on the mode and manner of feminine dress. Biblical evidences suggest that Hebrew women normally clad themselves with undergarments, outer tunics, robes and cloaks as well as head dresses and veils[20] while Christian women were also commanded to :

'adorn themselves in modest apparel, with shamefacedness and soberity: not with broidered hair, or gold, or pearls, or costly array: But which becometh women professing godliness with good works.'[21]

At the time of the advent of Islam, man had already passed through a long and constant process of evolution and the wearing of clothes to cover one's nakedness had become a normal standard of observing modesty in most civilized cultures. Nonetheless, the exploitation of the female species by its male counterpart had reduced women to mere objects of sexual gratification and the mode of dress imposed upon women sought to please men rather than cover their nakedness and therefore it was a common practice for most women to appear in public with such scanty clothing as exposed a considerable portion of their physical beings. Islam considered this exposure imposed upon women by the perverted nature of their menfolk detrimental to the high social and moral standard expected of its flock and therefore a considerable improvement in the mode and manner of dress was found essential before it could be considered acceptable to the high standard of morality demanded in an Islamic civilization.

---

[20] Isaiah 4.20/23
[21] 1 Timothy 29.10

The Quran itself stated that God has provided mankind with clothing to protect it from the variable changes of weather[22] as well as to cover its nakedness and be a source of elegance:

'O children of Adam, We have created for you raiment to cover your nakedness and be a source elegance.'[23]

It therefore commands Muslims to guard their modesty with what God has bestowed upon them and stated:

'Say to the believing men that they lower their gaze and guard their modesty. That is purer for them. Surely Allah is well aware of what they do. And say to the believing women that they restrain their looks and guard their modesty, and that they display not their beauty except that which is apparent thereof, and that they draw their head covering over their bosom. and that they display not their beauty save to their husbands, or their fathers, or the fathers of their husbands, or their brothers, or the sons of their brothers, or the sons of their sisters, or their women, or such male attendents who have no desire for women, or such children who have no knowledge of the relationship between the sexes.'[24]

These Quranic injunction which require Muslims to observe modesty and dress in a proper manner and not expose their bodies or beauty to strangers has often been misrepresented to insinuate that Islam imposes an unnecessary burden upon women and proposes to keep them in seclusion with clothes

---

[22] Al Quran 16.82
[23] ibid. 7.27
[24] ibid. 24.31/32

that cover her completely. Nevertheless, such insinuations are neither supported by the content of the above Quranic passage which demands that men as much as women observe the rules of modesty nor are these supported by other verses in the Quran which cautions men not to expose themselves to women beyond the permissible limits and state:

> **'Successful indeed are the believers, who are humble in their prayers, and who shun all that which is vain, and who are prompt in paying the Zakat and who guard their modesty, except from their wives or those under their control for then they are not blameworthy; but whosoever seeks beyond that is a transgressor.'[25]**

Secondly, while Islam requires women not to display their beauty except that which is apparent thereof, it does not stipulate that women should cover themselves from head to toe and keep the veil on at all times.[26] On the contrary, Traditions settle the requirements of this injunction with the advice to the effect that:

> **'When a woman attains puberty, it is not proper that any part of her body should be seen except her face and her hands'[27]**

Incidentally, this mode of a respectable woman's dress prescribed by Islam continued to be an accepted mode of decency in the western society until late 19th century. History indicates that Victorian women of noble descent wore such dresses as exposed their faces and hands only but the overzealous dedication to the concept of individual liberty to

---

[25] ibid. ??
[26] Grant, Linda. Unveiling the New Muslim, Life & Times, 19 August, 1992
[27] Sunan Abu Daud

do as one pleases and not as one ought brought with it the breakdown of conventions in the present century and the predominantly Christian west began to take pride in exposing as much of its modesty as certain prejudices in the society would permit. Since the old schools fought a losing battle, the Western went so far beyond the previously accepted standards of modesty that it in the present age it has become fashionable to flaunt one's nakedness in public. Happily however, the brides of Christ - the Christian nuns - not driven by this passion to expose their beings to lustful eyes have retained their balance of mind and to this day continue to observe the traditional norms of modesty in their dress which does not differ much in detail to the dress Islam demands its women wear. Yet it is ironic that while Christian nuns are looked upon with respect and dignity by the western masses, a Muslim women becomes a subject of mockery to the same people.

Ironically, the complicity with which this entire issue is approached by the western world is often found shocking. The proponents of a woman's right to display as much of her body as it pleases her consider such a right to be a basic and fundamental right of an individual. They also consider the exposure of their nudity by women to be a sign of advancement - the breaking away of the civilized world from the traditional rules of modest and the taboos of the primitive era. Yet, when such exposure falls on their own doors, they take grave exception to it - a fact beautifully illustrated by the furore created in recent times when a member of a European nobility was exposed by the press to have failed to conform to the traditional rules of modesty expected of the nobility.

Incidentally, Islam does not imposes its standards of dress upon women alone but admonishes men as much as women to wear a decent attire.[28] It forbids men to wear certain types

---

[28] Sahih Bukhari 72.8

of clothes[29] as unnecessarily exhibit their physique[30] and demands that they take particular care not to expose certain parts of their bodies.[31] It also stipulates that men wear such dress as covers their limbs and it sets a standard for men to cover those parts of their body as are below the naval and above the knee.[32] Traditions indicate that the Prophet of Islam[sa] did not consider it proper for men to expose their chests[33] nor did he find it proper for them to expose their thigh.[34]

SEXUAL APARTHEID NOT PROPOSED

It has also been suggested that Islamic ordinances which require Muslim women not to expose their modesty to strangers imposes a form of sexual apartheid upon women who are never permitted to be seen by a man who is not a member of her immediate family. But this view is once again not supported by the Quran which permits women to appear before:

'such male attendants who have no desire for women, or such children who have no knowledge of the relationship between the sexes.'[35]

The closing sentence of this Quranic passage is in itself evidence of the fact that the only purpose of these injunctions is to safeguard both men and women from being excited with lustful thought and since it is within the nature of a man to be more easily excited at a woman's physical endowments and women are physically much weaker in strength to ward

---

[29] ibid. 74.42
[30] ibid. 72.21
[31] ibid. 8.10
[32] Sunan Dar Qutni
[33] Sahih Bukhari 52.143
[34] Sahih Bukhari 8.12
[35] Al Quran 24.32

off any forceful attempt on their chastity - they are particularly cautioned to bar all such avenues which might threaten them. Therefore, they are admonished not to display their beauty except to those within the permissible limits which not only includes their immediate families but also their male attendants and children who have yet not acquired the age of puberty and therefore do not pose any threat.

An assertion that Islam proposes to isolate women from men to the extent that they are not to permitted to be seen by a man who is not a member of her immediate family is also negated by the fact that Islam permits foster relations of a woman to enjoy the same degree freedom in her home as they would enjoy in their own homes. It gives the husband of a foster mother similar rights as it gives to the woman's own fathers[36] and brothers of the foster father are treated by Islamic law as uncles.[37] Since according to Islamic thought, foster relation puts within the realm of permissibility all those things which are permissible in blood relationship[38], Islam does not impose restrictions upon women appearing before their foster relatives.[39]

Another evidence which suggests that these rules of decorum have not been imposed by Islam to isolate women from men but have been devised as a necessary steps to eradicate the possibility of any form of illicit relationship is indicated by the fact that women in a Muslim household are also advised to observe the same rules of decorum in the presence of other women who are either not their relatives or a part of their household[40] since Islam does not consider it permissible for women should look at the nakedness of other women[41] or

---

[36] Sahih Bukhari 62.22
[37] ibid. 73.93
[38] ibid. ??
[39] ibid. 62.23
[40] Al Quran 24.32
[41] Sahih Muslim

else touch another woman's body except in a manner permissible to them.[42]

Nonetheless, in this relation also Islam has not singled out women since its ordinances demand that Muslim men should not keep staring at women but deflect their look away from them.[43] It cautions men not to cast a second glance at women outside permissible limits for the first may be casual but the second is bound to be intentional and therefore evil in nature.[44] Traditions also indicate that according to Islam, a first casual glance at a woman outside the permissible limits is pardonable while the second is positively prohibited.[45] These rules of decorum are not only to be observed when men are in the company of women alone but men have been given instructions to observe a certain mode of conduct when amongst people of their own gender also and not look at the nakedness of other men.[46]

These evidences should therefore establish that the purpose of these injunctions is not to create a form of sexual apartheid and isolate women in the sense in which it is often argued but its entire wisdom revolves around creating a healthy environment in which it is possible for men and women to safeguard their chastity and morals - an environment which may not be possible if a free intermixing of both sexes was tolerated or permitted. This does not however entail that women are totally prohibited from any kind of a permissible liaison with men outside the permissible limits. While Islam does not permit strangers to meet people of the opposite sex in seclusion[47] it does not deny them a right to meet each other in the presence of a person they are not legally entitled to

---

[42] Sahih Bukhari 62.119
[43] Sahih Muslim
[44] Jami of Tirmidhi
[45] Sunan Abu Daud
[46] Sahih Muslim
[47] Sahih Bukhari 62.111

marry.[48] Islamic ordinances also permits meetings between men and women as long they are not secluded from people.[49]

SEGREGATION OF SEXES

Islam no doubt requires the segregation of the two sexes to an extent that it forbids a free intermingling of men with women who are strangers or vice versa but all such injunctions are designed to eradicate the possibly of covert relationships being fostered in an Islamic society - such covert relationship which men of understanding in the Western world themselves admit is a form of human impurity and abuse of physical faculties and also a squandering of self, a betray of one's self and one's partner.[50]

The failure of the Judaeo-Christian world to observe these restrictions in its society has brought consequences of grave danger to the very structure of its civilization. Every taboo attached to extra marital sex has been discarded and free sex has to a great extent become the norm. In a recent survey conducted by the Gallup organisation in the United States, it has been reported that fifty one percent of Protestant admitted that they engaged in sex outside marriage. It was also reported that fifty three percent Catholic and forty nine percent Protestant students owned up to sexual activity with more than one partner.[51]

Yet another study conducted in the United States finds that only twenty percent of all unmarried women in their twenties are still virgins and a survey conducted by the National Institute of Health in 1983 reported that of all single women in their late twenties, four million had lived outside matrimony

---

[48] ibid. 62.112
[49] ibid. 62.113
[50] Hildebrand, Dr. Dietrich von. Purity
[51] Gow, Haven Bradford. Defence of Chastity

with a man at some point in time.[52] The deplorable consequences of this freedom has brought extreme pain in the western society. For instance, according to a report by the American Social Health Association, some twelve million Americans are affected by some kind of a sexually transmitted disease. In 1988 only, one million Americans contracted gonorrhea and about half a million new cases of genital herpes appear each year with the virus currently affecting an estimated thirty million people in the United States. The country is also stated to be overwhelmed with as many as one million teenage pregnancies every year.[53]

In the United Kingdom, the state of affairs is not any better. Statistics report that in the year 1990/91, as many 593,728 new cases were seen by genito-urinary diseases in England alone - a figure representing an increase of 27,772 over the previous year. These statistics are stated by official documents 'not to show the true incidence of sexually transmitted diseases as around ten percent are thought to receive treatment elsewhere than the National Health Service Genito Urinary Medicine Clinics.'[54] The number of notified legal abortions in England were recorded at a staggering figure of 160,189 of which 106,298 involved single women and 17,750 were widowed, divorced or separated women. The incidence of notified legal abortion for children under the age of consent is reported to have been as much as 2,994 while 29,583 teenagers between the ages of sixteen and nineteen, 50,444 women under twenty four and 59,606 in their late twenty's and early thirty's terminated pregnancies in England alone during the year 1991.[55] Statistics also report that of the 706,140 live births in England and Wales during the year 1989 as many as 199,999 were outside marriage of

---

[52] Duin, Julia. Purity makes the Heart Stronger
[53] Gow, Haven Bradford. Defence of Chastity
[54] Department of Health, Summary Information, SM12B, 1990/91
[55] Office of Population Censuses & Surveys, OPCS MOnitor, AB 92/4

which 250 conceptions were reported to children under the age of fourteen, 1,765 to children of fourteen and 6,367 to children fifteen years of age. It may be naive to deny the fact that that such deplorable conditions exist in the Western world on account of its prided standard of free movement and inter mixing of the two sexes without any restriction - a fact admitted by some of the greatest western scholars who maintain that:

'With the growth of freedom there has come a much greater opportunity for conjugal infidelity than existed in former times. This opportunity gives rise to the thought; the thought gives rise to the desire and in the absence of religious scruples, the desire gives rise to the act.'[56]

Why then should Islam apologise for the acute wisdom with which its members, both men and women, are preserved against this physical pain and humiliation which has plagued billions of men and women with disease and often physical disablity and also with humiliation and grief?

THE VEIL AND ISLAM

The donning of a veil by Muslim women has often been a subject of ridicule in the western press and not only non-believers but also some converts to Islam allege that veiling is a male distortion of medieval theology exploited to keep women in their place[57] and therefore Islam needs a Reformation in order to allow the light of reason into superstitious beliefs and habits with no contemporary rationale.[58] Nevertheless, such a view has absolutely no place

---

[56] Russel, Bertrand, Marriage and Morals
[57] Saba Risaluddin, vide. Unveiling the New Muslim, Life and Time, London, Aug 19, 1992
[58] ibid, Linda Grant

in Islam nor is Islam in need of a reformation to suit the acceptability of outsiders since the view that the purpose of the veil in Islam is to hold women in subjection to men has most likely been borrowed and misconstrued from the Biblical rationale which maintains that the veil is a sign of female subjection to men:

> **'a man indeed ought not to cover his head, forasmuch as he is the image and glory of God: but the woman is the glory of the man. For the man is not of the woman; but the woman for the man. Neither was the man created for the woman; but the woman for the man. For this cause ought the woman have a veil on her head because of the angels.'[59]**

On the basis of this commandment in the New Testament, Christian scholars of repute have argued that:

> **'a veil on the head was the token of subjection and respect to superiors; if a man, therefore, should pray or prophesy with such a covering, he would dishonour Christ his head, by acting out of character, and appearing as if he was placed in subjection to the woman, instead of in authority over her. On the other hand, it would be inconsistent with modesty and her state of sunjection, for a woman to lay aside her veil on such occasions; for thus she wuld seem to forget her place, and to affect , which would dishonour a man, whom God had appointed as a head over her.'[60]**

---

[59] 1 Corinthians 11.7/10
[60] Scott. Illustrated National Family Bible, p. 1105

Islam does not subscribe to the view that the veil is a sign of female subjugation to men nor does it require women to wear a veil merely to satiate a man's alleged desire to hold women in subjection. This is evident from the Quranic injunction:

> **'O Prophet! direct thy wives and daughters, and the women of the believers, that they cast down their outer cloaks from their heads over their faces. This will make it possible for them to be distinguished so that they may not be molested.'[61]**

The closing sentence of this Quranic passage is in itself an evidence of the fact that Islam requires women to don a veil as a precautionary measure so that they may be distinguished as respectable women and not be unnecessarily humiliated or molested by strangers. There is absolutely no suggestion in this Quranic passage, as it is to be found in the Biblical passages, that a veil is a sign of female subjection to men and it is therefore thoroughly unwise of Christian converts to Islam or other non-Muslims to impose a Christian rationale on Islamic injunctions.

This custom of women not exposing themselves to the gaze of strangers by donning a veil is neither unique to Islam nor is it new to civilization. The use of the veil by respectable women has been a universal practice among all nations. Even the Spartans who permitted their maidens to appear in public without a veil required married women married not to appear in public without a veil.[62] In Biblical history itself, Sarah, the wife of Abraham who had been forcefully taken by the king of Gerar was 'reproved and admonished by Abimelech to be

---

[61] Al Quran 33.60
[62] Bibliotheca Biblica, vol. 1

more circumspect for the future.'[63] She was advised by the Philistine king to cover her face with the veil[64] so as to:

'protect herself from impertinence and also guard her modesty.'[65]

This indicates that the Phillistines also considered a veil essential to safeguard women from the unnecessary gaze of strange men as did the Aramaeans since Rebecca who later became the wife of Isaac donned a veil[66] as did Tamar, the daughter in law of Jacob's son Judah.[67] The descendents of these two grand female progenitors of the Hebrew race also donned the veil[68] and women in the exclusively Christian congregation were also required to wear one.[68] Modern Christian organisations, hoping to justify their present conduct, explicitly against the injunctions of their sacred scriptures have argued that this Biblical verse requires women to wear a throw around as a wrap and not a face veil.[69] Nevertheless, Christian scholars of integrity have admitted that while in this instance, neither sacred nor profane writers use the word to denote a veil, yet all agree it means one here.[70] The New Testament is extremely insistent that Christian women ought to wear a veil and states:

'Every woman that prayeth or prophesieth with her head uncovered, dishonoureth her head: for that is even all one as if she were shaven.'[71]

---

[63] Poole. Illustrated National Family Bible, p. 20
[64] Genesis 20.16
[65] Poole. Illustrated National Family Bible, p. 20
[66] Genesis 24.65
[67] ibid 38.14
[68] Isaiah 3.23
[69] 1 Cornithians 11.10
[70] Aid to Bible Understanding, Watch Tower and Bible Tract Society, Penn. p. 468
[71] MacKnight. Illustarted National Family Bible, p. 1105

Saint Oaul who devised the rules of conduct for the Christian congregation took such exception at women discarding their veils that he demanded:

'If the woman be not covered, let her also be shorn: but if it be a shame for a woman to be shorn or shaven, let her be covered.'[72]

Christian scholars have considered such action by women who threw away their veils even while praying to be an imitation of heathen priestesses in their rapture.[73]

WISDOM OF DONNING A VEIL PROVED IN HISTORY

The wisdom of wearing a veil as a precautionary measure has often been proved in history and women who did not sufficiently safeguard themselves by donning one ran the risk of being molested and humiliated by complete strangers. For instance, Sarah, the wife of Abraham - the grand progenitor of the Hebrew race and the spiritual mother of the entire Judaeo-Christian nation was taken by Pharoah's men because she captivated the Egyptians with her beauty. She was brought to Pharaoh's palace where his officials praised her beauty also and Pharaoh took her unto himself as a wife only to find that she was a married woman.[74]

Yet, even after her release by a God fearing man, Sarah did not to learn a lesson from the disastrous situation in which she had found herself and put her husband - only because she chose to displayed her beauty to strangers in public and not don herself with a veil which was an accepted standard of observing modesty in her own land from whence she

---

[72] 1 Cornithians 11.5
[73] ibid 11.6
[74] Genesis 12.14/19

travelled to Egypt[75] She continued to appear before strangers without a veil and consequently bewitched yet another powerful king with her beauty. Abimelech, the king of Gerar took Sarah as a wife as Pharoah had previously done only to be warned by the Lord in a dream that she was another man's wife.[76] Abimelech is also stated to have reproved Sarah for not wearing a veil and also informed her that he had given her husband Abraham a thousand pieces of silver[77] for him:

'to buy veils for thee, and all that are with thee, to cover thy face as it is usual for married persons to do.'[78]

Sarah was therefore reproved and admonished to be more circumspect for the future[79] but she failed in her duty to impress upon her family the wisdom of wearing a veil. He son Isaac having failed to learn an essential lesson from the two humiliating experience of his mother nearly put his wife Rebecca in a precarious situation. Rebecca, who had traditionally donned a veil while in her father's home[80], somehow appeared without one after she became a wife of Isaac. She enchanted the Philistines with her beauty and Abimelech the king of Philistines who had previously been bewitched by the beauty of her mother in law, Isaac's mother Sarah had to issue orders to his people not to touch Isaac's wife lest they be condemned to death by the king.[81]

Dinah, the daughter Jacob was however not as fortunate as her grandmother Rebecca. When she left her home without a veil, Shechem the son of Hamor the Hivite, prince of the country, saw her, took her, lay with her and defiled her much

---

[75] ibid 38.14
[76] ibid 20.2/12
[77] ibid 20.16
[78] Poole. Illustrate National Family Bible, p. 20
[79] ibid
[80] Genesis 38.14
[81] ibid 26.7/11

to the grief of her father and brothers who later proceeded to butcher every Hivite male in cold blood and take their children and women captive.'[82]

Had these Biblical women observed a proper and a befitting mode of dress and not flaunted their beauty for men of good character to be bewitched or men of perverted nature to be infatuated with lust by their assets which nature had endowed upon them - they would not have either found themselves in a precarious situation nor would they have been defiled and humiliated much to the grief and anger of their menfolk who apparently resorted to, in one instance, extreme violence which cost a nation the lives of its entire innocent male population and which brought captivity and bondage to their innocent children and women. This tragedy does not take into consideration the burden of sin which a naive woman thrust upon the shoulders of her brothers who in their grief and humiliation lost balance of their minds and resorted to deceit and mass slaughter of innocent human beings - only to bring further grief to their father.[83]

The purpose of purdah in Islam is not to unnecessarily restrict the movement of women or else keep them in seclusion as virtual prisoners within the four walls of their homes as often argued by some either out of ignorance or else sheer prejudice against Islam. This is indicated by the Quranic passage itself which states:

'O Prophet! direct thy wives and daughters, and the women of the believers, that they cast down their outer cloaks from their heads over their faces.This will make it possible for them to be

---

[82] ibid 34.1/31
[83] ibid

distinguished so that they may not be molested.'[84]

Had Islam placed any restriction on the movement of women or forbidden them from leaving the four walls of their homes then this Quranic passage which requires them to don a veil to protect them from the gaze of strangers would have been found to be superfluous. Nevertheless, there is absolutely no denying that women in Islam have not been given a license to wander outside their houses without due cause or justification.

Islam recognises the physical and psychological differences between the male and the female species and it also acknowledges the capabilities and limitations of men and women. It therefore designates distinct roles to them - appropriate to their innate abilities and aptitudes and also strengths and natural inclinations. The Quran states in relation to this:

'Our Lord is He Who endowed everything with its appropriate faculties and then guided it to its proper function.'[85]

It is in view of this diversity of creation and function that women have primarily found themselves responsible for the domestic welfare of their families and the administration of the household while their menfolk have borne the responsibility of providing for the material need of the household. But this neither diminishes a man's responsibility to assist women in the household nor does it deprive women the right to assist their menfolk in providing for the household needs.

---

[84] Al Quran 33.60
[85] ibid 20.52

The history of early Muslims is full of instances where Muslim men assisted their wives in ordinary household chores while Muslim women went out of their homes to assist their menfolk in whatever manner possible. The Prophet of Islam was himself not only eager to help his wives at home but he often assisted them in the household chores.[86] Women on the other hand were encouraged to come out of their homes to participate in such projects as were beneficial to the welfare of the community[87] and also other festivities.[88] They were commanded to attend religious functions[89] where some sections of the Muslim society placed unnecessary restrictions on their womenfolk leaving their homes, they were advised against such a practice.[90]

Muslim women assisted in the battles fought by Muslims during the lifetime of the Prophet[91] as well as the succeeding caliphs.[92] They nursed the wounded and the sick and even carried the Muslim martyrs back to Medina.[93] Some even excelled in the battlefield as did 'Asma bint Yazid[ra] and Umm Ammarah bint Ka'b[ra] who actually took up arms in the battlefield. Others engaged in sea battles as did the wife of the then ruler of the Muslim empire, Mu'awiya[ra] and also Umm Haram bint Milhan[ra], the mother Anas ibn Malik[ra], one of the greatest scholars known to the history of Islam.[94] The wife of Prophet Muhammed[sa], Ayesha bint Abu Bakr[ra] led Muslim men of such intellectual capability and high military reputation as Talha ibn Ubaidullah[ra] and Zubair ibn Awam[ra] into the battlefield.[95]

---

[86] Sahih Bukhari 11.44
[87] ibid 15.20
[88] ibid 62.76
[89] ibid 8.28
[90] ibid 15.20
[91] ibid 52.65
[92] ibid 52.65
[93] ibid 52
[94] ibid 52.68
[95] ibid

Muslim women also assisted their husband to supplement the household income and also worked in farms.[96] Asma bint Abu Bakr[ra] collected date stones from her husband's fields some six miles from her home and Zainab bint 'Abd Allah[ra], a skilled craftswoman supported her husband and children.

Muslim women prayed behind men[97] and regularly left their homes to attend prayers at mosques before dawn and after sunset also[98] although their husbands, often such powerful puritans as Umar ibn Khattab[ra] disliked might dislike it[99] but would not stop them[100] since Prophet Muhammad had commanded men not to deny their wives a right to come to the mosques to offer their prayers.[101]

During the period of the second caliph, Umar ibn Khattab[ra] who had previously taken exception to his wife going to the mosque to offer her morning and evening prayers placed the supervision of the markets throughout the Muslim domain in the hands of women.

DISTINCT ROLES DEVISED BY NATURE

Nevertheless, this does not alter the fact that God has fashioned mankind according to the nature designed by Him and there is no altering in the creation of the Lord.[102] He has equipped women with certain exclusive faculties and capacities which make them more suited to a domestic role - far above what a man could ever expect. For instance, she has been equipped with the capacity to conceive and bear children and neither science nor the most dedicated

---

[96] ibid
[97] ibid 13.38
[98] ibid 12.28
[99] ibid 8.13
[100] ibid 13.11
[101] ibid
[102] Al Quran 30.31

exponents of the modern concept of women's liberation would ever be able to alter the course of nature. Women have also been equipped endowed with the capacity to suckle their off springs and as yet the nutritional value of breast feeding has neither been matched nor replaced by modern substitutes.

In His infinite wisdom, the Lord has also endowed women with better and finer emotional capacities which make them an ideal species to cope with the stress and strain of domestic administration. It has also been admitted that in human psychology, women represent the being in whom reside all the most energetic and powerful sentiments of pity, affection, altruism and devotion.[103]

But, the exponents of a woman's absolute parity with her other half in every sphere of life are totally blinded by their prejudices and refuse to accept the ultimate fact that nature has endowed the two species with such a diverse physical and psychological constitution that any attempt to fuse the realm of their activity would be totally against the laws of nature itself. Women of great caliber have themselves admitted that differences existing between men and women do not merely come from physical diversity or the mode of education but are of a deeper nature but that the ignorance of fundamental facts has led many a feminists to believe that both sexes should have a parity in all spheres of life. However psychologists have themselves admitted that:

> **'In reality woman differs profoundly from man. Every one of thecells of her body bear the mark of her sex. The same is true for her organs and above all, of her nervous system. Physiological laws are as inexorable as those of the sidereal world. They cannot be replaced by human**

---

[103] Guyan, J.M. Education and Heredity

wishes. We are obliged to accept them just as they are.'[104]

Such women scholars of human psychology who have excelled in their field far above many men in their profession have then advised women to:

'develop their aptitudes in accordance with their own nature, without trying to imitate the males. Their part in the progress of civilization is greater than that of men. They should not abandon their specific function.'[105]

The part played by women in the progress of civilization is no doubt much greater than that of men. It is an admitted fact that the social fabric of the world has been built around the womenfolk of our society.[106] Men have no doubt been required to provide for the material needs of the family but it is women who fashion the future of their offspring and ultimately the society. With them has rested not only the future of their children but also nations and mankind itself[107] since women possess in them the power to endow their offspring with a good constitution, a vigorous intellect and good morals and in them rests the power to alter the structure of their children for weal or for woe.'[108] But a proper discharge of her duties as mother with whom rests the future of the world and the power to alter the structure of the future generations imposes certain limitations to a woman's freedom. The neglect of these duties by a woman can have grave consequences on the upbringing of her future generations.

---

[104] Carrel, Dr. Alexis. Man, The Unknown
[105] ibid
[106] Mason. Women's Sphere and Primitive Cultures
[107] Stetson, Charlotte Perkins
[108] Bayers, U.S. Maternal Impressions

Islam is thoroughly aware of the finer capacities and the better capabilities possessed by women and influence women can exercise in the constitution and structure of the future generations. Therefore it designates the sacred trust of domestic administration to women them and requires them to primarily restrict themselves to their duties at home. But this does not mean that Islam proposes to either hide them or seclude them from society. Women have been given the right to pursue their own vocations within the confines of modesty and decency - provided these vocations are not pursued at the cost of their primary duty.

The whole essence of the Islamic teachings relating to the concept of purdah proposes to inculcate modesty within a society and therefore save women from the kind of humiliation to which they have been subjected before the advent of Islam. Hence the Quran admonishes women:

'Stay in your homes with dignity, and display not your beauty in the manner of the women in the days of ignorance.'[109]

WISDOM OF QURANIC INJUNCTIONS YET PROVED ONCE AGAIN IN HISTORY

The wisdom of the Quranic injunction requiring women to observe a proper code of morality by not displaying their beauty like the displaying of former days has been tested and proved by the events of history. Women who either ignored their duties at home and unnecessarily wandered away from their security of their houses or else women who failed to observe the rules of modesty within or without the four walls

---

[109] Al Quran 33.34

of their houses have often found themselves in the most unfortunate and distressing situations.

It has already been shown that Abraham's wife Sarah who displayed her beauty to strangers brought consequences of great enormity upon herself as well as her husband and also the Egyptian ruler and his household. She put herself in a similarly precarious situation once again when she displayed her beauty in public in the land of Philistines which consequently brought a great sin upon the king of Gerar, Abimelech and his kingdom. Her daughter-in-law Rebecca also enchanted the Philistines with her beauty and would have found herself in a precarious situation were it not for Abimelech's near fatal experience with her mother in law, Sarah.

Dinah, the daughter of Jacob was defiled because she choose to leave the security of her home. Homor the Hivite who violated and humiliated her did so because he was deeply attracted by her physical beauty which she had not taken any care to conceal from the gaze of strangers. A renowned Christian scholar commented upon the fate that befell Dinah to state that women:

'must learn to be chaste keepers at home.'

Tamar, the widowed daughter in law of Jacob's son Judah left the security of her parents' home to bring consequences of great evil, shame and humiliation upon herself and her deceased husband's household. She dressed herself like a harlot and drew her father in law into committing incest with her. As a result of this willful act of fornication, Tamar was rightfully accused of 'playing the harlot and being with a child by whoredom.' She was nearly burnt to death by her father in law's orders but for the fact that she had conceived an illegitimate seed which belonged to him personally. Tamar who played the harlot to her own father in law brought forth two illegitimate sons which shamed the household of her father as well as that of her father in law.[110] This would have never happened had Tamar been content to 'stay in her home with dignity and not displayed her beauty like the women in the former days of ignorance.' A Christian scholar commented upon this incidence in the Bible to state:

'Those have eyes and hearts too full of adultery that catch at every bait that presents itself to them, and are as tinder to every spark. We have need to make a covenant with our eyes, and to turn them from beholding vanity, lest the eye infect the heart.'[111]

This is exactly the covenant which the Quranic injunctions in relation to purdah proposes to establish in an Islamic society. A covenant which requires Muslims to turn their eyes from beholding vanity lest their hearts be infected and consequently their bodies be defiled and their souls damned. But Islam does not leave this matter in abyss. It devises hard and fast rules to enable mankind from avoiding the pits which can lead men and women into eternal damnation. It requires women to stay in their homes with dignity[112] and not display their beauty like the women in the former days of ignorance.

The dignity which Islam requires women to observe is achieved through several ways. They are required to restrain their eyes from looking at men outside the prohibited degrees; guard their modesty; not display their beauty except that which is apparent thereof; draw their head covers over their bosoms while within the four walls of their houses or places of work.[113] They are also required to cast down their outer cloaks from their heads over their faces so that they are

---

[110] Genesis 38
[111] Commentary on the Whole Bible Volume I (Genesis to Deuteronomy) By Matthew Henry
[112] Al Quran 33.34
[113] Al Quran 24.32

not harassed or molested by strangers[114] but where women have passed the age where they could be molested, the Quran gives them permission to lay aside their outer clothing without displaying their beauty.[115] Finally, Muslims women are required not to be soft in speech lest in whose heart is a disease should be tempted.[116]

The application of these injunctions is not restricted to women alone. Men within a Muslim society are obliged to retrain their looks and guard their modesty as much as the women are obliged to restrain their looks and guard their modesty[117] as well as wear a decent dress which does not expose their physiques unnecessarily.[118] Men as well as women are required not to look at the private parts of the each other, whether they be of the of the other species or their own kind.[119] Therefore Islam does not impose a singular burden, if any, upon women. But, within the scope of their activity, it also requires men to observe the rules of decorum - the rules of decorum Sarah, Rebecca, Tamar and Dinah failed to observe and hence found themselves drawn into the snares which not only put them in precarious situations but also humbled them and their families.

These rules of decorum, Islam insists, are to be observed within the four walls of a Muslim home as much as outside and such injunctions of the Quran which demand a universal application of these rules are not without wisdom. For instance, the Biblical David and Bathshba's failure to observe these essential rules of decorum and modesty within the four walls of their own homes resulted in them being driven into committing sins of grave proportions. Had Bathsheba been more careful in the manner in which she conducted her life

---

[114] Al Qurran 33.60
[115] Al Quran 24.61
[116] Al Quran 33.34
[117] Al Quran 24.31
[118] Bukhari 8.10
[119] Sahih Muslim

within the confines of her home, David would not have had the occasion to observe her stunning beauty from the roof of his palace. On the other hand, had David himself been more careful with the manner in which he spent his leisure time within his own palace, he would not have permitted himself to gaze into the private courtyards of other people's homes. Consequently, he would not have had this occasion to observe Bathsheba washing herself within the four walls of her own home nor would he have been infatuated by her beauty.

But, David and Bathsheba disregarded the essential rules of decency - David by gazing into the private courtyard of other people's homes and Bathsheba by taking a bath in an open space from where she could be easily seen by a stranger standing on the roof of the king's palace. Their actions led to the grievous sin of adultery being committed by the couple and a seed of sin being conceived by Bathsheba. This sinfulness was further aggravated by the husband of Bathsheba, a gallant commander fighting for his king being slain by one of David's officers on the king's command.[120] Their actions had a grave impact upon their entire household and many years later, David's sons considered the conduct of their parents 'a licence to their youthful inclinations.' They concluded that he could not greatly censure them after he had set them such an example[121] and therefore, David's son Amnon who became infatuated with the beauty of his own sister Tamar forecfully violated her.[122]

While one does not accept the truthfulness of these Biblical events which dishonour the piety and purity of God Almighty's blessed servants, one cannot overlook the fact that these myths were given considerable currency by the Jews and the Christians at the time when Islam made its first appearance

---

[120] 2 Samuel 11.1/17
[121] Scott INFB pg 340
[122] 2 Samuel 13.1/14

in Arabia. It was therefore essential for God Almighty to Himself impose the rules of decency through which the righteous may save the physical being of Muslims from being defiled and their souls from damnation. The injunctions relating to purdah are but a mere safeguard from the Muslim nation falling into a pit which the Jews and Christians believe their nations fell into.